BLUE MOON

Finding Answers About Death Through
Ancient Wisdom and Modern Healing

Christine De Wan

TITLETOWN
PUBLISHING

TitleTown Publishing, LLC
P.O. Box 12093 Green Bay, WI 54307-12093
920.737.8051 | titletownpublishing.com

Publisher: Tracy C. Ertl
Editor: Lori A. Preuss
Designer: Erika L. Block

Names:	De Wan, Christine, author.
Title:	Blue moon : finding answers about death through ancient wisdom and modern healing / Christine De Wan.
Description:	Green Bay, WI : TitleTown Publishing, [2023]	Includes bibliographical references.
Identifiers:	ISBN: 978-1-955047-27-2 (trade paper) ISBN: 978-1-955047-25-8 (eBook)

Subjects:

LCSH: Death--Religious aspects--Christianity. | Children--Death--Psychological aspects. | Life change events--Personal narratives. | Mother and child. | Parental grief. | Bereavement-- Psychological aspects. | Loss (Psychology)--Religious aspects. | Spiritual healing. | Mental healing. | BISAC: BIOGRAPHY & AUTOBIOGRAPHY / Personal Memoirs. | FAMILY & RELATIONSHIPS / Death, Grief, Bereavement.

Classification: LCC: BT825 .D48 2023 | DDC: 236.1--dc23 Revised Standard Version Bible: Anglicized Catholic Edition, copyright © 1989, 1993, 1995 the Division of Christian Education of the National Council of the Churches of Christ in the United States of America. Used by permission. All rights reserved.

~ To my son Evan, whose life is an Everlasting story of Love

That reaches beyond the moon and stars ~

CONTENTS

CHAPTER ONE: IT WAS A BLUE MOON

By appearances, it seemed like an ordinary debut of a Fall Friday night with that elusive hint that Summer had just taken her bow and slipped gracefully away behind the curtain...almost unnoticed. That night, however, turned out to be anything but ordinary...*and what was about to slip away, was anything but subtle.* With no forewarning, we were standing on the precipice of a jarring, life-altering event that shook us to our core and changed us forever.

We had just returned home from a Friday night high school football game. As we pulled into our driveway, my husband Matt excitedly shouted, "Chris! Look at the moon! It's blue!" I remember us both getting out of our van, looking up, and noticing that it did indeed have a mysterious blueish hue to it. I had never seen a full moon quite like it. It looked magical, like a picture out of a storybook and we both paused for several moments together, looking up in awe. We were wonderstruck! I didn't know there was a special meaning behind a blue moon or what it meant, nor did I know blue moons would soon be showing up in peculiar places or that I'd be doing research on them. All I knew in that moment was the bedazzling beauty cast before us as we both gazed up into the starry night sky. It was a hallmark moment and the moon was to become a sort of talisman or true north compass point for us. We were about to discover answers to *many* questions–not just about the moon, but about life and healing after losing a child. Drawing on our faith and becoming more open to expanding our beliefs, our life and family endured many challenges and overcame monumental struggles *while experiencing divine encounters and numerous miracles.* And just as the moon rises every evening to shine its light in the darkest hours–Our Everlasting love for Evan still shines brightly in and through our hearts.

Well, I found out what a blue moon is and it's usually not blue in color except on very rare occasions when there may be matter suspended in the atmosphere due to a recent forest fire or volcanic ash from a recent eruption. The Summer of 2012 was the state of Colorado's worst wildfire season in a decade so maybe that had something to do with it. The saying, "once in a blue moon," refers to this rare combination and the effects of fire and the cosmos. After conducting more research on the internet, I found out a blue moon simply refers to the occurrence of a second full moon within one calendar month. There have only been 4 blue moons since August 31, 2012 (the night of Evan's accident) and the next blue moon is going to be on August 31, 2023.

Originally, in the early 1900s, according to such places as the Maine Farmer's Almanac, the term "blue moon" meant that four full moons occurred within a season, rather than the typical three. There is a lot of folklore around the whole blue moon phenomenon. There's even a widely popular Belgian blue moon beer (mango is my favorite!) and a company named Bridgeview has an Oregon Reisling wine by that same name. I have tasted them both.

Many songs have been written about blue moons or moons in general. The song "Blue Moon" has been recorded by many artists throughout the years and Andy Williams rendition of "Moon River" has always touched a chord deep inside my soul. "Fly Me to the Moon" (Tony Bennett) and "Moondance" (Michael Buble') also top my favorites list of classics. Even though it isn't about a moon, a song that is about a special time in September, "Try to Remember A Kind of September (when life was sweet and oh so mellow)" by The Brothers Four, is another old song I listened to growing up in a home where music was always playing. Now when I hear these old songs associated with the moon, especially in September, I feel a special connection with the other-worldly fleeting moments these crooners tried to capture in describing rare and boundless love. And I feel a vastness that's bigger than the relationship itself — of Evan's presence in the universe.

It seems appropriate to capture the visceral feeling I get inside when summer turns to Fall. It has *always* been my favorite time of year. Autumn is nature's way of transitioning us into new activities while providing a gorgeous backdrop of brilliant color. Mother Nature steers the course for us to follow and we adjust to her schedule accordingly! For me, it is sweater weather that brings the urge to get out my knitting needles. Just walking outside to drink in the beauty of leaves crunching under my feet brings joy and transports me back to my high school days of walking to school and cheering at football games. Everything has a crisp, sharpness to it. The Air, the leaves...even school schedules demand disciplined start times and homework deadlines. I love the rhythm of Fall after a somewhat slower languishing summer with beach visits, family camping, and lemonade sipping. Matt loves to watch high school football and Fall is the season when his work at Bay Valley Foods, better known as the "Pickle Factory," slowed down.

August 31, 2012, held that feeling of the "inner shift" I was experiencing that day as if the new season was changing inside of me too. However, the magnitude of the shift I was about to experience was literally cosmic. It was the evening of that day when I would experience my first "blue moon."

We had plans that night to catch a local high school football game. Our good friend's son played for Southwest who was playing against Ashwaubenon and it was perfect football weather.

At that time I was working part-time in corporate training at Northeast Wisconsin Technical College (NWTC) our local technical college. Our children were out of high school and at various stages of building and navigating their own lives. Our oldest daughter Erin is married and lives in De Pere with her husband Jared and their 2 children. She is my stepdaughter who has been in my life since she was 5. Matt and I got married when she was 7. We then waited 5 more years before having more children so there was a 12-year gap between Erin and the next three. Our oldest son Evan was now 24 and living in Madison while attending college at Madison Area Technical College (MATC) and working as a DJ. There are 18 months between Evan and Michael (Mike), who was now 22 and back living at home and working, after some schooling at the University of Wisconsin, Oshkosh. Our youngest daughter Ann – or Annie as we call her, just turned 19 in June of that Summer.

That Summer of 2012 was a worrisome time for us as parents of young adults. I was volunteering in youth ministry and after returning from a week-long middle school faith camp experience at Camp Tekakwitha in Shawano, I wrote the following excerpts in my journal:

June 16, 2012 (Ann's 19ᵗʰ Birthday)

"We have sacraments because God knows we need tangible things to help us understand invisible things and God gives us as many do-overs as we need. His mercy is endless and new every morning."

June 17, 2012 (Father's Day)

"Asking God to Bless Matt. Holiness happens one day at a time. Help us recognize signs of your blessings. Help us hear you calling to follow you. GO THERE – even if we can't see HOW it contributes to the <u>final product</u>. Jesus, I trust in You. Jesus, We trust in You. In order: Seeds/Open Doors/One step at a time/ Patience/Let go of worry/Trust in God/Do your best/Let God do the rest – for His plan and His final product to unfold and produce HIS good fruit. In order."

I have kept private journals since I was around 30. I guess I have always had a lot to say – to myself and God – who I believe is always listening to me. Writing words on a page helps me process life. I refer to these journals and rely heavily on them, especially now, to recall memories that have either faded or I have totally blocked out. Many prayers were penned and I began to notice that in a few days, weeks, or months later – those prayers would be answered.

So, what was I worried about that particular summer? Our 3 young adults were testing and navigating the waters of life and at times treading on the dangerous seas of our modern-day culture. I was really worried they were going to be swept away. I felt like they had forgotten their foundation and prayer and church were no longer important to them. Evan was making his way without any financial support from us, but we were concerned that some of his choices could carry heavy consequences that would harm his spirit and create a false sense of his divine identity that would trickle down and be modeled to his 2 younger siblings who looked up to him. Evan spent 2 years at UW Oshkosh (1 of those was with Mike) and I think it's fair to say we all know what UW "Sloshkosh" is well- known for – as well as many other colleges in our state and in general. The party scene can be quite enticing and distracting for so many young adults and ours were no exception.

Matt and I made the decision early on in our children's lives to be involved in an education that was based on faith values. We did our best to model our faith at home, though we were far from perfect. We prayed and researched the area school choices before finally deciding to send them to a catholic school. Matt did NOT have a good catholic school experience. When he was in 2nd grade his older sister witnessed him getting hit with a ruler for writing with his left hand. When their father, who was a public school junior high teacher, found this out, he had a meeting with the catholic school principal and Matt was moved to a public school. I, on the other hand, went through 6th grade at All Saints Catholic school in Gladstone, Michigan, and had a very good experience. I went to public school only because our catholic school had closed and there was no other option. We weighed our options based on both of our experiences, (1 good and 1 not so good) and decided we'd be actively involved and volunteer at the school of our choosing. We ended up choosing St. Joseph school. Of course, we were concerned about being able to afford the tuition for 3 children but we wanted them to have a strong faith-filled foundation and to know who Jesus was so that they would know who *they* are – *beloved children of God*. This was important to us.

The circumstances surrounding Evan's death left us with so much unfinished business. Matt felt guilty that he had not tried to spend more time with Evan – especially after our last Christmas together. In those nine months that fol-lowed, we reached the "expiration" date. Like food that you toss out because it has spoiled...it felt like such a waste. "We wasted that time," Matt said, but in my reality and speaking for myself, I was giving Evan the space he needed and I truly felt I was honoring his journey. Even though my heart was aching to recover our damaged relationship, I was waiting for him to make the next move. About 1 week before the accident, however, I did reach out to Evan. I called him on the phone. I remember I had just finished work at NWTC and I was sitting in my car in the parking lot. Evan answered his phone and after asking him how everything was going, I told him everything at home was not going so well.

Ann had recently been to Madison to visit her big brother and I wanted to talk to him about setting a better example for her. I asked him to confirm something for me. I wanted to know if there were some adults (and I named names) who had been influencing all 3 of them throughout their teen-age years and even up until now, in regards to drinking and smoking. He validated what I had suspected. I told him I respected his honesty with me and I meant it. He knew that I thought partaking in this lifestyle would not lead to good things, but I told him respectfully that it's his life to live, not mine. I said that the younger two looked up to him and that *HIS* influence was having a great impact on their lives – affecting *them* and affecting *us as parents.* It was a short conversation and uncomfortable, but it was good to hear his voice.

Evan always told the truth. I may not have liked what he said, but I always respected that he was honest with me. We always say "I love you," before hanging up, and that was the end of our conversation. My intention of this call was not to go on a witch-hunt of who to blame for our family dysfunction – I believe in free will and we all make our own choices in how we choose to live. My intention was first of all to connect with Evan and keep the line of communication open and to see who I could trust and who I wanted to surround myself with to have healthy relationships moving forward.

This was my last conversation with Evan. It was the first time we actually spoke to each other since the "Christmas incident." It still wasn't the "good" bye we all hope for when coming to closure with the death of a child or loved one. This was our last goodbye, but I just didn't know it. Until a week later.

"Lord, I surrender all my worries to you today. I need your healing touch. You say, BE NOT AFRAID. I am trying Lord." This was my journal entry written on Sunday, July 1, 2012. It was the last entry written until my next journal entry which was on that surreal day, Labor Day, September 1st, 2012, which **affected us ALL** forever. It was that Saturday we learned that Evan lost control of his car while driving home from a DJ gig and was instantly killed…under the light of a Blue Moon.

Matt was the Quality Assurance Manager for Bay Valley Foods in Green Bay and he took turns working Saturdays right alongside his staff. He never felt superior to them and wanted to work just as many Saturdays as they were all expected to work. This was his Saturday to work. While things typically slowed down in Fall, September could still be a very busy month for processing pickles and so he was up by 5:00 am and off to work for 6 on that Labor Day. Sometime shortly after 7:00 am our doorbell rang – jolting me out of bed. I threw on my bathrobe and scurried down the hall to the front door. Through the window I could see a policeman standing outside. I immediately felt my stomach turn inside out. My first thought was that something happened to either Ann or Mike who were still living at home.

I opened the door and the police officer politely asked if I was the owner and if my name was Christine De Wan. I said I was. He asked if it was ok to come in and then proceeded to ask if Matthew was my husband, to which I also answered "yes," but explained that he was already off to work. He then asked where Matt worked and I told him the Pickle Factory which was about 1 mile from our home. The officer explained he needed to talk to both of us together and then proceeded to send another officer to Matt's work to inform him to come home right away. My anxiety just ramped up a notch.

While we were waiting for Matt to come home – which seemed like an eternity – I invited the officer to sit down in our living room. It was quiet and awkward. Ann and Mike were still sleeping in their rooms – the doorbell obviously did not disturb them. The police officer was a young man. He was very respectful and calm as he sat across from the sofa where I was sitting.

At that time I had a large picture of Jesus hanging on the wall above the sofa. He commented on the picture and said his dad was a preacher who had that exact same picture hanging in his office. It was probably only 10 minutes before Matt walked through the door accompanied by the officer who was sent to retrieve him. Matt immediately asked what was going on in the most serious tone of voice I've ever heard him speak. I could tell he was trying to brace himself. I was bracing myself too. I'd seen enough television drama shows that when this scene unfolds with a police officer coming to make an announcement – it is very bad. Matt sat down next to me on the sofa.

The officer asked if we had a son named Evan who lived in Madison. We both said, "yes." That's when he said, "This is the least favorite part of my job."

That phrase epitomizes the meaning of "looking like a deer in the headlights," because it was the pin-pointed moment of no return. He then said, "Your son Evan was killed instantly in a car accident around 2:00 am this morning." After bracing and holding my breath, I let out a gasp and felt a gut punch like I've never felt before.

My brain was trying hard to process the words that were just spoken out loud. From that moment on, the rest of that day and for weeks to come, was like living in a dream where when you wake up, you only remember bits and pieces and nothing makes sense. I was in such a state of shock, I started to cry and said "Oh my God," as I lowered my head and covered my face. Matt did not cry because he was shell-shocked. It was so conceivably unbelievable to comprehend.

Next, the officer handed Matt a slip of paper with the name, title, and phone number of the medical examiner on it and the name and phone number of the attending officer at the scene of the accident. He instructed Matt to first call the examiner to identify Evan's body. Matt got up, went into the kitchen, and called the number. When the medical examiner answered she asked Matt if he could verify any specific markings on the body that would confirm this was indeed our son. Matt explained that Evan had a tattoo on his right forearm that was a piano keyboard with his mother's name, "Christine" written across the keys. Check. I'd like to imagine she expressed her sympathy. She said our son was killed instantly due to traumatic injuries. Blunt force trauma to the head, chest, and lower extremities.

Matt hung up the phone and relayed the information to the police officers and confirmed to them he had identified Evan's body. (Matt later called the attending officer at the scene and the next day we drove to Evan's apartment where the officer talked with Matt and gave him all the details of the exact location of the scene. He even mapped out the scene with the trajectory the car took from beginning to end. I chose not to go and witness this. I did not want to sear any branding images more horrifying than the ones I already had in my mind, but our son Mike went along with Matt a day or 2 later. The car was removed, but there was still debris -- bits and pieces of metal/plastic scattered from Evan's car.)

The young officers expressed their sympathy again and said not to hesitate to call if we had any questions – and they left. *I wonder how the rest of their day went?* I shut the door behind them, my head still reeling and my body stunned and numb. I couldn't understand how this could be happening and if it was even real.

Matt immediately went to wake up the kids and tell them the news. He went to Ann's room first and she started crying right away and came into the living room by me. I was sitting in a bewildered state of disbelief and I was starting to get frantic now. She started asking a million questions and all I could do was pass on what was reported by those kind officers, repeating the details over and over. When Matt went into Mike's bedroom Mike didn't believe him at first, so he had to repeat that "Evan was killed in a car accident last night." Mike followed Matt into the living room where we all were now, stunned and in shock and still under the watchful eyes of Jesus above us sitting on the sofa. We had to repeat to Mike the same few facts we knew about the accident – facts we would have to repeat over and over to so many people who were consoling us in the days and weeks that followed. Repeating these bits of information somehow gave us *some little shred of Evan to hold onto.*

There was a very eerie feeling that accompanied this living room scene. You would think under the circumstances we'd all be hugging and crying together. But in our shock – we were all processing the news in our own ways and within half an hour Ann and Mike left the house seeking consolation from their friends, and Matt drove to De Pere to share the news with Erin.

It was when she opened the door and by the look on his face, immediately asked him what was wrong, that he broke down and started to cry. He was gone for a long time because as he told me when he got back home, he stopped at Newcomer's Funeral Home to talk to someone who could help him. That's when he met Megan, the young gal who would end up taking care of us during our time of crisis. She was an angel and just the person we needed.

Alone and at home, I started making phone calls. Devastating news travels fast, especially with social media. It didn't take long for everyone we knew to feel the tremors of the shock waves that were reverberating out from our house in all directions. These actions of spreading the news were instinctive. There was no thinking about what we each needed to do. There was just the doing. Receiving this earth-shattering news and then calling people kept my panicked mind busy – like I was tossing a rope out to keep from being swallowed up from going into the deep abyss from the cracks that were forming underneath the very spot I was standing on.

Before long, word was out – like lightning speed. Evan had SO many friends from Green Bay, Oshkosh, and Madison. Andy, his best friend growing up, came over to the house about the same time my sisters arrived and he hugged me so tight. Said he heard the news and called his parents (our friends) immediately who were camping out of town. Evan spent a lot of time at Andy's. Andy was a shining star for us that day. He introduced himself to my sisters and started helping out. To this very day, Andy calls or texts me EVERY Mother's Day, holiday, Evan's birthday, and the anniversary of his death. We also make a point at least once a year to visit or grab dinner together. He calls me "Mom." Friends like Andy are rare and true blue. True Blue Moon, I'd say.

Towards the early evening of that Labor Day, one of my closest friends–Mary–came over and walked with me around our neighborhood. Her steady presence kept me grounded and her listening ear was gently cradling each word and detail I shared.

Exhausted from the *labor of the day,* before going to bed that night, I found the energy to write one sentence in my journal.

September 1, 2012: "Our precious Evan John De Wan died this morning shortly after 2 am...he was killed in a car accident in Madison where he lived."

CHAPTER TWO: FROZEN IN TIME

Evan was a gifted musician. He took piano lessons in grade school and guitar lessons in high school. For his 16th birthday, we pitched in half the cost of a Special Faded Gibson electric guitar–with the agreement that on his birthday he would play for us the song he was working so hard to master in his lessons... "Stairway to Heaven."   He had been practicing for months and he delivered on his promise to an audience of our family plus Grandma and Grandpa De Wan in our living room after dinner! I have to admit – he really rocked it! I thought it was too much money for a birthday gift, but Matt overrode me on this and Evan came through on his end of the bargain. He played it flawlessly.

I took music lessons the opposite of Evan. In grade school, I took guitar, and later as an adult I took piano lessons. Music was always playing in our home, either on the stereo or on the piano. For a long time, we had 2 pianos in our large living room. One was a digital Yamaha Clavinova. That was the *sweetest* instrument ever! You could record and overlay sounds of other instruments and sound professional even if you were just a mediocre musician like me. You could even go back over and correct any mistakes and we could play the recorded music in the background as if listening to the stereo. Maybe that's where Evan got his inspiration for DJing and the recording arts.

Evan continued playing music through high school, was in Jazz Band, and formed his own band with friends. Evan took his love of music with him to UW Oshkosh with dreams of getting a recording arts degree.

During his first year of college, he got a tattoo on his right forearm. We didn't allow any piercings or tattoos while in high school (under age 18) even if you were in a rock band. His tattoo was a piano keyboard that took up most of his right forearm. *And he had my name, Christine, signed beautifully over the keys!* How can a mother be upset with this? I was very taken aback – I did not like tattoos, but I have to say it was done tastefully. I kidded with him that I hoped he and I never got mad at each other because he'd be staring at my name every day for the rest of his life! The thing is, we didn't get mad at each other, at least not for very long. Yes, we disagreed about things, but Evan was respectful toward us and always honest with his answers. Even when we didn't like the answers he gave. The respect was mutual.

I will always have this image in my mind of Evan as a kind of eclectic mixture of band beatnik, and computer geek. He built his own computer and was a gifted musician. He was a highly motivated and goal-oriented young man, and he was very frugal, too. Second-hand clothes and furniture were his preference. I think maybe Breezi rubbed off on him because the first question she asked me when we met was, "Do you recycle?" Breezi was his first (and I really think his only) real true love. Yes, Breezi is her real name, and it fits because she's light as a whisper and free as a bird. She's a petite little thing, yet VERY strong. She is a teacher, a serious championship hula-hooper, and clothes designing entrepreneur. She's a twin, which is super fun. I don't know where or when she and Evan met exactly, but we were introduced to this lovely little spitfire of a gal the summer before Evan's 2nd year of college – her first.

Our first introduction to her was not exactly a pleasant one. Evan thought it would be ok if a bunch of his friends crashed at our house in sleeping bags after a late night of fun, disrupting our household – and I kicked them all out!

The next day Evan apologized and told me about Breezi (who was with the group the previous night). I explained the "proper" way he should introduce his father and I to a girl he was deciding to date. He listened and set up a day for Breezi to come over, and he properly introduced her to us in our living room. We instantly liked her and could see how happy Evan was to be with her.

Evan had lots of girl FRIENDS in high school but had his heart broken a few times with dates either turning him down or standing him up. I remember one girl called him about 4 hours before the homecoming dance and said she had to go to her uncle's funeral. (Lame) I felt SO bad, a little piece of my heart broke for him, but he made the best of it and joined up with some of his other friends, and off he went. He didn't seem to wallow too much – He just moved forward. I admired that about him. Evan and Breezi stayed together through the year at Oshkosh and then they saved enough money to move to Madison, which was their dream. They got engaged to be married sometime in 2010, but eventually, they parted ways, yet remained good friends. They supported each other, and to this day I consider her my "daughter-in-law." She will ALWAYS have a special place in our lives.

Evan had a way of drawing people together. Once he moved away, he never really asked for anything. And he never looked back. He seemed to enjoy his self-sufficiency– and that allowed him to play the game of life by his own rules without any interference from the folks. That's how it seemed to me, and actually, I had no problem with that because isn't that what we all want for our young adult children? If he wanted advice, he'd ask for it. If we gave advice, he listened respectfully, but ultimately he was supporting himself financially and making his own decisions. Decisions... decisions...

While in Madison and after the breakup with Breezi, Evan was doing more DJing and mixing and recording his own music, which was what he LOVED doing most of all. But Breezi later shared with me that he was not happy with the direction his life was taking, and felt he wasted some valuable time. She went on to earn and finish her degree and Evan started back to school at Madison Area Technical College in that Summer/Fall of 2012. He only got to attend the first couple weeks of classes when he had his accident. We were not aware that he was experiencing some depression. In fact, I didn't find out until a few years later, when I confirmed this information with Breezi after having had a Medium reveal it to me in a class I was taking. So, while we didn't interfere with Evan's independence, we also were not aware of the deeper stirrings of his life. That made me really sad and I always wish we could have had that "friend" relationship I talked about earlier. We never got there with Evan.

The last Christmas before the accident, Evan came home for the Holiday break. Matt drove to Madison to pick him up for the weekend. Christmas was on a Saturday that year and the Packers were playing in town at Lambeau Field. Personally, I am not a fan of the NFL for having games on Christmas day. Yes, I understand that Thanksgiving has always been a football tradition, but games played on Christmas day rivals precious family time. We live in Green Bay and actually live about 5 blocks from the stadium, so we are definitely impacted by "game day" with all the parking, tailgating, and partying. After having a nice and relaxing, lazy Christmas morning together and exchanging gifts, our sons, like so many others who live here, partook in the pre-game festivities. Then they went to a few bars that night together and came home very late, feeling no pain and quarreling with a tag-along friend, who was looking to pick a fight. (Although this friend was SO drunk, he could barely stand up, much less be a threat to anyone.)

So, on this Christmas night in the wee hours of the morning, Matt and I got up because of the noisy disruption. The best we could do to diffuse the situation was to get our sons in the house and call the police to see if they could get this other young man (who was now stumbling around in our neighbor's yard) safely home. The police came and took care of the young man, and we all went to bed. Having to call the police on Christmas night (well actually it was now the 26th) was not the "Silent Night, Holy Night... Sleep in Heavenly Peace" ending to Christmas of 2011 that I would have preferred.

Very early the next morning, Evan's ride back to Madison came to the house to pick him up. We didn't know of his plans to leave so early, but apparently his friend had to get back to work. It was an awful morning and his leaving not only felt abrupt but left the incident from the night before hanging with all kinds of ugly loose ends trailing. Evan left without saying much to any of us. I'm sure he wasn't feeling very good about the damper it left on Christmas and our family time together. It was the last time Matt and I saw Evan alive. I'm not sure if it was for Erin, Mike, and Ann. There was unresolved business and layers of dysfunction underlying that Christmas holiday. The drinking culture in Wisconsin and raising children in that culture was always an issue for me. I discovered that many parents hosted parties for their high school teens because "at least I know where my kids are and I can control and monitor the situation." Personally, I think some parents just want to be their kid's "friend" which is a cop-out for the responsibility it is to be a P-A-R-E-N-T, in my opinion. When our kids started high school and I found out how prevalent this behavior was, I started calling parents out and even paid one a visit...but it didn't make much of an impact and was HIGHLY unpopular. Except maybe now... my kids will always know that I was not vying for their friendship or out to win a popularity contest to be the "coolest" mom – I was their MOTHER. Friendship would come later, hopefully with respect for standing my ground and speaking my Truth.

So this was the backdrop to the story of our last night together as a family. From here we just kept moving forward with our busy lives, not really addressing any issues...just waiting for the next disruption to happen...ringing in the New Year of 2012 to see what would await us next.

CHAPTER 3: UNDERSTANDING GRIEF

The words Evan and I didn't say in that last phone conversation were, "I'm sorry."

The weight of the guilt of those words NOT spoken was almost more than I could bear. You would think in a time of crisis, we would have all pulled together as a family. We didn't. Evan's death shattered us. Into fragments. I came to realize I couldn't "fix" everyone else's pain and what they were going through in their own grief journey, but I kept searching to find some closure and healing for my own. Somehow, by the grace of God, I was led to doing my own inner work, and that's how I gradually discovered healing. It has taken me a long time and I have only begun to scratch the surface of trying to understand grief while being a member of the "losing a child" club. My understanding of grief in that space is unique to me. Your understanding of grief will be unique to you, however there are some universal similarities. There is no word yet to my knowledge of what you call parents who have lost a child – except perhaps, "childless," but that doesn't quite fit because that term refers to parents who prefer not to have any children or are *unable* to conceive a child. There is a term for children without parents, and that is "orphans." And that's rather pitiful, isn't it? What child wants to be labeled an orphan? Maybe it's best if there isn't a label. I think I like it that way. Label-less. We get to be who we are – and stay that way. P-A-R-E-N-T-S. Nobody can take away our Parent-Badge. I still wear mine proudly. I'm still Evan's Mother, as well as Erin's, Mike's, and Ann's Mother. Nobody can take that away from me and nobody can take it away from you either. And for that matter, nobody can steal the JOY we experienced from having our children in our lives, even if it was for a short time. Our joyful memories WAY outnumber our painful ones! Did you know we still carry their DNA in our body? Yup, look it up.

About 2 years after the accident, while trying to understand and make sense of my "new" life without Evan, a trusted co-worker/friend explained energy healing to me and invited me to give it a try. She told me she intuitively thought I'd be open to hearing about energy healing or Reiki. I had never heard that word before, much less know what it was. I was now working part-time as a youth minister and a friend from another parish sent me an email and on the Subject line it said: *"A Personal Visit."* She then went on to explain that the Spirit was leading her to talk with me about "your son and daughter." She said our conversation would be happening because I was open to it (whether or not I realized it.) She said she was being led to share a gift with me that she doesn't often use and only with a few other people who knew about it. She apologized for the "cryptic" feel of the information in the email, but would I want to meet with her sometime soon? She said I could name the time and place. She ended with, "May our Loving God continue to bless you and your family."

I realize now that she was taking a great risk in sharing with me that she practiced reiki. Her career – her job – her income would be jeopardized if word got out that someone working for the catholic church was going around offering reiki to people. My response to her was immediate. I didn't think her message was cryptic or creepy in any way. I trusted this individual. Even though I didn't know her extremely well personally, she worked in ministry for a very long time and she was very intelligent, funny, and respected among her peers. In my new position, I had the honor of getting to collaborate with her on several events and retreats. I instinctively knew she probably had a message for me from Evan, and I trusted that whatever she had to share with me would be good. In my email response to her, I asked if we could meet the next day after work at the Allouez Cemetery at Evan's gravesite. I explained that it is very peaceful and quiet there. I said I would bring a blanket and we could sit under the shade of the young silver maple tree.

She responded back in another email and said the cemetery meeting place was perfect and she thanked me for allowing her to use her gifts. She said our gifts should only be used for life-giving and that sometimes the life-giving part comes after what doesn't feel too good. She said, **"Patience is a key ingredient."**

When we met the next afternoon, my friend explained to me that she sees and hears "others" in spirit. She asked me if I had ever heard of reiki healing… and she explained a little of what it was about. She encouraged me to do some research on it. She said she practiced reiki and if I wanted I could come to her house and have a session with her to experience it. She said it might be helpful in healing my grief. This is not the first time I experienced someone with such gifts. I knew another lady (catholic) who also had gifts of seeing and hearing spirits. She was a member of a funeral choir I belonged to many many years ago and had given me a "message" from the Holy Spirit one day after choir practice. The message was from Revelations 21:5, "Behold, I make all things new again." Along with this Scripture message she said she saw a flower with all the petals fallen off except for 1. I thought this was a lovely message for me and I took it to heart even though I didn't know what it meant for me at the time. My life was pretty good back then. Ironically this old acquaintance sang in the choir for Evan's funeral and after Mass, she told me she had a message for me which ended up including having 6 Masses said for Evan to release him from purgatory. In my state of shock I welcomed this message, but as time went on it did not resonate with me. It felt extremely rigid and "conditional." I do continue to pray for our loved-ones-passed, but for now we'll focus on understanding grief through my learning about energy healing.

My reiki friend modeled her faith and now she was offering her gift of healing with me. The fact that she receives messages from "others" from the other side gave me HOPE and felt life-giving to me without the "let's make a deal aspect attached to it like some conditional clause." The message Evan had for me was to think about what my friend was telling me about reiki. She encouraged me to do some research on it and then make a decision based on that. And so I did some online research and I met with my friend 2 more times at her home to ask her more questions about our catholic faith and what the church teaches about this "new age" sort of healing. I finally had a peace about trying this reiki healing and I had my first ever energy healing reiki session on Tuesday evening of September 23, 2014 – almost 2 months after we met at the cemetery. She answered all my questions and I had done my research along with prayerful discernment. I did not go blindly or naively into this session. And at no time did I ever feel forced to try it. I was trying to reconcile my life and all my relationships and this all began to happen with me being OPEN to listening to a message from our son Evan. My friend was also discerning when the right time was to approach me. Later when I started using my intuitive healing gifts – I used this same approach with my son Mike. I had to wait until he was ready and OPEN to receiving a message from his brother – and this in turn helped him on HIS healing journey. (We all have intuitive gifts if we are willing to take the time to listen and be open!)

Very simply put – Reiki is an ancient Japanese form of the "Laying on of Hands." Like ALL energy healing, it is intended to facilitate a relaxed state of being for the recipient's body so they can participate in the healing process. I ended up having several reiki sessions with my trusted and gifted friend and through each session different areas in my life that needed "work" and heal-ing – were revealed to me in loving ways. As I was learning to LOVE MYSELF (not carry around a lot of guilt, especially in regard to my relationship with Evan) and do my "inner work," I was also learning to meet people where they were and not where *I* was on the journey. As I was learning to honor my own healing journey of grief, I was learning to honor and respect the others in my family. In one of my early sessions, I saw (in my mind's eye) the outline of Evan's face, like it was traced with connecting stars against a dark, indigo-col-ored night sky. I literally felt his face pressing against mine and I could feel tears gently and tenderly seeping into my ears while at the same time, I heard the words, "I'm sorry for all the pain you're going through." I heard them and felt the vibration of those words touch my heart in waves of love that are hard to describe. I was sorry too – that I didn't make more of an effort after that Christmas to reach out sooner than I did. Saying my part out loud allowed the heavy burden of guilt to be lifted from my shoulders.

Now 11 years have gone by and while I still don't understand everything, I do understand this – a lot of healing has taken place not only in myself, but our entire family has come together in new and miraculous ways. We have ALL had some form of energy healing and I trust that the unfolding will con-tinue. What my friend said was indeed true: "sometimes the life-giving part comes after what doesn't feel too good" and ***"Patience is a key ingredient."*** I couldn't fix the other's pain – I could only work on my own and take responsi-bility for the role I played. I think now about the words of the song, "Let there be Peace on Earth, and let it begin ***with me.***"

Aspects of my faith expanded, and this flowed outward and helped the dy-namics of our family structure change...for the better...as I changed and healed, so did they. Each in their own time and way. And we are still healing. In a combination grounded in our faith, through energy healing and connecting with Spirit/our loved one(s) – we were *still able to communicate our "I'm Sorry's,"* our *"I miss you's"* and *"I'm thinking about you."*

The unresolved or unfinished business got some resolution and the beginning of that healing was being able to forgive and accept forgiveness – especially with myself. If Love Never Ends and can't be taken from us, can't we reciprocate forgiveness from both sides of heaven and earth also? Forgiveness leads us to a deeper more authentic love, so how could this energy healing be a weird thing? I believe I can still forgive someone who has died – and by a story, I will later share with you about how Evan guided me to give his brother Mike a message, tells me our loved ones from Heaven can still ask for and forgive us too! I'm convinced of it. I think this is how we achieve Peace On Earth. One healed relationship, one piece/peace, one step, one person at a time. Then let God do the rest of the math and multiply…so it flows…like a river…flowing out from you and me…flowing out into the desert…setting ALL the captives free.

This fun little fact just came to my mind: I live on LIBERTY street. My healer friend lives in FREEDOM. Freedom and Liberty. Don't you just LOVE it? Peace my friends.

So that is how I started my journey to becoming a facilitator of healing which took nearly 10 years and it all started because a brave intuitive healer friend of mine, for whom I am *eternally grateful*, took a daring, compassionate risk and approached me with sharing her gifts back in 2014. Hey girlfriend, if you are reading this, I hope you feel *the love.*

The biggest, deepest gaping wound had been inflicted upon all of our hearts. It's been 11 years now and we are all at different stages in the healing process. There's a saying, "You never get over it, you get through it." Or the flipside is, "you don't." How do you even begin to heal a broken heart especially when losing a child? I know God was listening to the questions I had in mine.

Three weeks after the accident on September 22nd, my dear friend Anne came over to do a house blessing ritual. We went through each room and sprinkled holy water and said some prayers together. The air and energy in our home seemed so thick and heavy. I gave away all the funeral plants because they were a constant reminder of sadness for me. I was just trudging through my days. I had been off from work at NWTC for 2 weeks since the accident and this was the end of my first week back. Doing this ritual was like a sacramental blessing. We did it ourselves. Didn't need a priest. I felt better momentarily. I have known Anne for a long time. I met her when she answered my day-care ad for her two beautiful girls. I remember the moment Evan started reading. He was sitting with Anne's older daughter in our stuffed rocking chair when Greta called me over to show me how my 5-year-old was reading the story with her help. I hadn't seen Anne for a while because now our kids were grown, but I was so grateful she popped back into my life, sharing her gifts and knowing just what I needed at the moment. That night I was talking to Evan in my mind and wrote this to him in my journal: "I don't understand God's plan, Evan. I need to take better care of myself and I'm not sure what I should be doing." "I've suppressed my anger and it has not been good for me – depression."

Elisabeth Kubler-Ross is the world-known Psychiatrist who developed the 5 stages of grief theory. The 5 stages are *Denial/Anger/Bargaining/Depression/ Acceptance*. Later on, David Kessler co-authored 2 books with Elisabeth called, Life Lessons: Two Experts on Death & Dying Teach Us About the Mysteries of Life & Living and On Grief & Grieving: Finding the Meaning of Grief Through the 5 Stages of Loss.

The 5 stages don't necessarily happen in order and are not reserved for death. We can experience these stages as we go through any kind of loss. David Kessler added a 6th stage of grief and that is *Meaning*. David explains that your loved one's life had meaning and purpose and it affects the meaning of our lives too. David lost a young adult son to a drug overdose. His loss is different than mine and different than yours. Our son lost control of his car which caused it to crash so badly that the jaws of life had to retrieve him. Our losses are all unique to each of us, but it's comforting to know how to navigate the stages by reading what others have shared from their experiences.

Denial is usually the first normal response we have and it acts like a "safeguard" to the initial shock we experience at hearing the announcement of the death. Denial helps us to cope and make survival possible. Denial helps us to pace our overwhelming feelings of grief. When we start to ask ourselves "why" this happened, we are beginning to move into healing, beginning to slowly feel some of our feelings. Denial fades gradually when we are ready to start feeling our feelings.

Anger can last a very long time because we'll have a million things or people (including ourselves and God) to blame for our loved one being gone. Though uncomfortable, anger can be a sort of anchor to hold onto rather than the empty nothingness we'd rather not feel, so it's healthy to let it surface. It's also helpful to seek counseling or join a support group such as *The Compassionate Friends,* an international support group for parents who have lost children.

Bargaining is the game we play in our mind that consists of the "what ifs..." or "had I done..." statements where we create different scenarios that could have caused a different outcome for our loved one. This stage allows our guilt to surface so we can face it and deal with it. This is especially a stage we place ourselves in when a loss is due to a chronic or terminal illness where we are holding on to prayer and miracles.

Depression is the 4th stage Elisabeth describes as another necessary phase in experiencing dying and loss. It is an appropriate response to a deep loss. We withdraw from life for a time, feel confused as if wandering in a fog and we may even wonder why we are here anymore. It would be unusual for someone to not be depressed when suffering from the death of a child or beloved.

Acceptance is the 5th stage and like the others, doesn't happen all at once. It happens in bits and pieces as we learn to adjust to our new reality of life without our child or loved one. It does not mean that their death was o.k. and that we are fine. The death will never be o.k. with us because we are forever changed and will always feel a loyalty to our loved one. We can never replace what was lost, but we can learn many new things like investing in our current relationships and for me, finding alternative ways to help deal with my pain. I found many new friendships with people who have also suffered terrible losses in their lives. Their authenticity helped me with finding mine.

Meaning is the 6th stage of grief that David Kessler added to the 5 established by Elisabeth, and one that takes us full circle. Our loved one's life *mattered* no matter how long or short their time here on earth was – even if the child involved was the result of a miscarriage. Every life matters and has meaning to us and sharing the life and loss of that child or loved one with others honors them **and** it honors a part of us that once was. Simply put, it honors the love. Meaning can be a way of bringing closure as well as honor to the love each life carried within. My life was deeply impacted by Evan and this book shares the depth of that impact and what he taught and continues teaching me about life. Our relationship has NOT ended. It has just taken on a different form.

As a child, David witnessed a mass shooting as his mother was dying in a hospital. He grew up and became the world's foremost expert on grief and loss and that's when he tragically lost his 21-year-old son. I'm grateful for people like David who have shared their stories and helped so many countless others who have and are struggling with devastating loss.

I love this stage of meaning – it helps everything else make sense. Our loved one is gone, but our love for them actually grows stronger. I think that's pretty amazing how God made our hearts that way. David Kessler is a very strong courageous man and God has entrusted him with a lot. He and so many others are beacons of light for us to grab onto when we're swimming in a sea of darkness.

I think I started processing Denial, Anger, and Bargaining (with God) when I began to realize I had to let go of the fact that when I started raising teenagers I could no longer schedule, monitor, or control every facet of their lives like I did when they were dependent on me and Matt.

Shortly after Mike was born. I ended my 10-year job in accounting at St. Vincent Hospital and started my own home daycare business. At that time, I was relishing in the innocence of being home with small children all day long. (H-O-M-E is my favorite word) I remembered once hearing some people at a church event talking about those "troublesome teen years." I secretly thought to myself, *"how tough could it be?"* My children were so well-behaved, had excellent manners, and were so heartwarmingly sweet! I think I was already practicing for the DENIAL stage. Thinking that somehow *my* children wouldn't get into any trouble. I just couldn't imagine it. That was either really naïve or super egotistical. Probably a combination of both as I see it now. It wasn't too long before my 16- and 17-year-old darlings started testing the waters of their independence and moved into those turbulent teen years full steam ahead where they had freedom and outside influencers. I no longer could control the environment as I did in my home day-care setting. I was the one getting "schooled" now.

Matt and I started to doubt our parenting skills. What were we doing wrong? I had a very low point while raising my teens and I want to share how it challenged and strengthened my faith. This was several years *before* Evan's accident. I remember the day – sitting in my "prayer room." We have built-in bookshelves in this room and I have an entire shelf dedicated to books of the Saints. I'm obsessed with them—always have been. Maybe a seed was planted when I attended All Saints School as a child. I don't know. So I purchased a new book from the Lighthouse Christian Bookstore entitled, "The Family God Uses." It seemed to be "calling out" to me. But when I read it, I wasn't impressed. It didn't resonate with me at the time. It was a story about a family that had some struggles and, in my assessment, ended up with a fairytale "happily ever after" ending. It seemed unbelievable to me and actually, kind of lame. A "too good to be true" story. I re-shelved the book.

Around that same time, Evan made the decision not to get confirmed. He told us (very respectfully) that he still considered himself a Christian but was making his own decision not to get the sacrament. More "**DENIAL**" kicked in… we were deeply invested in volunteering at St. Joe's. Matt and I were teaching 9th grade religious education. (I actually did the teaching; Matt says he was my catholic "bodyguard" to keep law and order in the classroom!) Now we had other worries. Will our other 2 children follow Evan's decision not to get confirmed? What will our catholic peers think? We felt like failures…but after the initial shock, we came to accept Evan's decision and Evan did go to the Mass for the Confirmation Ceremony – because I *asked him to* and because I was his best friend Andy's confirmation sponsor. I wanted Evan to celebrate Andy's special day and he did and was very considerate about it. I was learning to accept and acknowledge that my children were learning and growing, and I was learning to honor and respect their journeys…and not judge them. I will tell you, however, as a fiercely devoted mother…I ramped up prayers over our children like never before. (BARGAINING?)

My main worry in all of this teen-age messiness was really not whether or not they went to church or received the sacraments – but whether or not they would pull away from God and their faith. I didn't even care if they pulled away from me. (Well maybe a little) I use to pray what I call the Scary Mom's Prayer: "Thank you God for the gift of YOUR children. Lord, they are not mine, they're yours." If they are doing something that is hurting them, stop them in their tracks."

If they didn't want God in their lives – what direction would they be headed in? I'm not sure how many people are aware of this but did you know that Wisconsin has been dubbed the Drunkenest State in the nation with UW Oshkosh and UW Madison ranking at the top of this category? Some years back, the Green Bay Press-Gazette did a month-long series about the Culture of Drinking in Wisconsin. Evan was heading off to Oshkosh and I knew the day we dropped him off for move-in, was the day I finally had to cut the strings and let him go. I accepted that we had done the very best we could as parents. I cried on the way home knowing that I had let go of a piece of my soul. It was a different feeling than what I heard other parents say about their experiences of children going off to college for the first time. I KNEW our relationship was going to take a different kind of turn. It seemed to have a *finality* to it. Sometime later, sitting in my prayer room again, feeling frustrated, abandoned, and alone, I got that book down from the shelf (The Family God Uses) and I said to myself, "Not my family," *then I threw the book in the trash.*

I think dropping Evan off that day at Oshkosh was a kind of ACCEPTANCE stage. I knew in my heart our relationship changed and I truly did let him go. I was not a hover parent once any of them left the house. In the house—another story—my house, my rules. But what you do outside my roof is your choice and your consequences.

So, I think when it came time for dealing with Evan's death – I went straight to DEPRESSION. I was already on a low anti-depressant a few years leading up to the event due to shoving my feelings down and not dealing with them, but now I went into full-blown clinical depression. There is a difference. My mind had shut down and I ended up quitting my job at NWTC. In fact, I withdrew from everything and went into a deep dark place.

CHAPTER 4: MOURNING FOR YOUR CHILD

According to Jean Galica, M.A., Licensed Marriage and Family Therapist, death, in any case, is hurtful and painful, but a child has a significant role in bonding and bringing two partners closer together. When that bond has been disconnected through the death of a child, its effects can significantly impact the relationship between the parents of that child. Trust between 2 married persons is the VALUE that gets tested the most in experiencing the death of a child. According to Jean, the profile of a grieving couple has 4 major issues that couples reported resulting from the death of their child: 1) sexual problems, 2) emotional distance, 3) more conflict and/or fighting, and 4) if the child was the glue that held their marriage together, they need to find a new foundation. Dr. Galica does not cite any percentages of marriages that end up in divorce under these circumstances.

I agree with Dr. Galica not citing any "statistics." Statistics can plant ideas or seeds in people's brains. People are not statistics. Though it may be interesting to see what those divorce statics are, there is most likely an underlying, unresolved issue at the root cause of divorce under these circumstances. Matt and I attended a couple's retreat one Valentine's weekend a few years after Evan's death. It was a lovely time together. It was held at Saints Edward and Isadore in Little Suamico.

As part of the program, we watched a video where there were different scenarios of what causes stress in a marriage. One of those segments was about a couple who had lost a small child to drowning in the bathtub. It was a heartbreaking story but very informational and got our attention. The narrative shared a statistic that around 80 percent and higher of marriages end in divorce after the death of a child. That is a very high percentage. I had grandparents who lost a young adult child (their oldest daughter Ann, whom my youngest daughter is named after) also in a fatal car accident. Back in those days, divorce was not very common, but they did end up separating. They did however have deep respect for each other. As a child growing up, I could plainly see this through their actions. I believe they did not have the available resources and other family support they needed to express and process their grief. I hope my similar experience brings them JOY in heaven as they witness the work of Evan's love through me to be a part of our family's legacy of healing.

Whether you are married or a single parent, Dr. Galica further states in her findings: "Grieving is some of the hardest work an individual ever does. It is a coming to terms with the fact that, in this instance, your child is dead, one who loved you back, whose needs once gave shape and focus to your days. You can never have your child back, he/she is not just on a trip, they cannot be replaced, what the parent wants most they cannot have, because their child is gone forever from the face of the earth. It is final! If parents do not grieve the loss of their child, they will stay frozen in their pain. They must now build a new life in which the child does not live, but they also need to keep the child *alive in their hearts and memories.* The parent tends to be left with more pain and to have a harder time coming to terms with their loss, the more conflicted the relationship was between them and their child." (www.jean-galica.com)

In another article entitled, THE MYTH OF DIVORCE FOLLOWING THE DEATH OF A CHILD (3/1/2015) Stephanie Frogge helps dispel the myth of the death of a child being the cause of a high percentage rate of divorce. In that article, she cites several other studies to back up her findings. One such study is the following.

According to a 2006 study conducted by The Compassionate Friends, an organization that supports bereaved parents, the divorce rate among couples that suffered the loss of a child is about 16%, not the 80-90% which they believe is a myth that people have been *"conditioned"* to believe from other sources. In a 2017 article from Psychology Today, Susan Pease Gadoua, L.C.S.W. writes that the loss of a child will stretch you, but divorce is not inevitable and depends on *many* factors. The top 4 are:

1. How strong the relationship was before *the loss*
2. The cause and circumstances *surrounding the loss.*

3.   Coping skills each person had *before the loss.*
4.   How much support the couple gets.

Obviously, if the relationship was weak prior to the tragedy, the loss could be the straw that breaks the camel's back. One or both partners may have been looking for a reason (consciously or subconsciously) to leave and this paves the way to exit. Resentment and blame for other issues in the relationship can rise to the surface and a child's death can be the catalyst to set things in motion.

From my own experience, losing my child undoubtedly tested our marriage. If the marriage is set on a solid foundation, even such a tragic event as losing a child will not *cause* that foundation to crack. If the marriage ends...it's most likely due to stress cracks that were already there. At the time we were going through our loss, we didn't realize that our foundation was being tested... but it most definitely was and here we are 11 years later and getting ready to celebrate our 40th wedding anniversary on October 7th. (Which happens to be the feast of the Rosary which Matt prays EVERY day.) Foundations. Good stuff. Our foundation was not made of sand. Poured concrete. Nothing is gonna damage it. Not. Even. Death. I will say, however, that we were ALWAYS working on our marriage throughout the years. We attended many marriage retreats that I believe helped shore up our "cracks" when they started *before* they were beyond repair.

Once you belong to the "I've lost a child" club, you meet other parents who have endured the same test. The majority of couples we've encountered have remained married, with the exception of a few. In our experience, surviving Evan's death reinforced our foundation, rather than destroying it. I'm not judging divorce either—my parents were divorced. They are/were both excellent parents. It happens. Sometimes it is the best option because we are all doing the best we can.

In this hardest of situations, the best thing we can do is walk THROUGH the darkness of it. If we walk around it, we will spend our lives frozen or walking in circles. I believe death is more openly talked about now and there are so many more resources available and ways of finding healing now than when my grandparents suffered the loss of their daughter Ann. After Evan's death, my mother shared some things about how her family was affected by Ann's death. Ann Kathryn Almonroeder was the oldest of 7 children of my grandparents Gust and Julia Almonroeder. She was almost 20 when she was killed instantly in a car accident. My mother Nancy was the next oldest. She was 16 years old at the time and was the one to receive the "phone call" announcing the accident. About a week after Evan's funeral, my mother came for a visit probably to check on me...and she said she was amazed at how well I was holding up. (I wasn't really – still in shock) She said after the death of Ann, "grandma" (her mom) didn't come out of her bedroom for around 6 months, except to cook dinner while the kids were at school. After preparing food grandma would go back to her room. My mother said grandma came very close to having a nervous breakdown. My mother, being the next oldest in line took on the role of mothering. My grandparents owned a tavern that served food, so grandpa was probably trying to keep that going without grandma's help. They eventually lost the tavern...lost their home...and went their separate ways. Grandpa went to work on the ore docks and grandma had to go to work too. She moved into a very small upstairs 2-bedroom apartment that her parents owned. She had 4 children yet at home, so the 2 boys had 1 bedroom and the 2 youngest girls shared the 2nd bedroom. Grandma slept on the sleeper sofa in the living room. She ended up working at a nursing home to make ends meet. She walked every day to and from work – neither of my grandmothers ever learned to drive, much less own a car.

My reason for sharing this with you is to illustrate how a previous generation in my family dealt with the tragic loss of a child in comparison to the resources we now have available to get help and healing. Listening to my mother share her family's experience helped me know a little about my history. It was heartbreaking for my grandparents and their family, but it shed light on my own darkness. It gave me more compassion for where we've been and helped me navigate moving forward. Here are several lessons we've learned in the past 11 years on how to cope while you are mourning the loss of your child.

1) There are valuable life lessons that come from experiencing pain. Never, never, NEVER give up hope. "...endurance produces character, and character produces hope." Romans 5:4. Talk to God/Source/ Spirit in your own special way – like when you're talking to your best friend. I'm bossy, and that's the way I sometimes talk to God. God

knows it. Ask for miracles. I always tell people, "If you aren't receiving miracles in your life, you're not asking." Just be careful what you ask for! God will blow the doors off your wildest dreams because God wants what you want too, only God usually outdoes our dreams.

2) Start at the beginning of what you know about faith. If you have lost your faith, START THERE. Admitting that you have lost faith, means that you once had it. Embrace and be ok with the fact that for a time unbeknownst to you...IT IS LOST. It's O.K. to be lost for a while. Go back to lesson #1 and ASK for someone to help you find your way again.

3) Find some sacred space where you can go to process and get away from the distractions of your everyday routine. Yes, life eventually needs to keep moving forward, but it took 9 months to conceive, plan and prepare for the birth of your child, and it's going to take longer than that to plan and prepare for a new life without them. In the Green Bay area, we have access to a Marion Shrine, Our Lady of Good Help. I spent many a day there alone and together with my husband. Retreat centers also offer places of refuge when nursing a broken heart. There is the Norbertine Center for Spirituality in De Pere, The St. Catherine of Siena Retreat House in Racine and Oshkosh also has a Jesuit retreat house available for both guided and silent time to process. Golden Light Healing in Sobieski (about 25 minutes north of Green Bay) is another place I was able to process a lot that I learned about energy healing as I struggled to reconcile it with my faith. ***And you can always count on me to listen to your story***. If I can't offer you the assistance you are looking for, I know many people now, who can. Helping Parents Heal is an organization on social media that may be a good place to land for some support and The Compassionate Friends have local chapters throughout the world. A huge part of you is missing and the ways to heal and the recovery time is different for everyone.

4) Everybody processes grief in their own way and at their own speed. The process cannot be rushed or forced. There are remnants of grief that never completely go away. They are pieces of our stories that deserve respect and honoring. They are anniversaries of the heart. Not ONE piece of your story should be shunned like biting into a bit-

ter sour apple. Your story is YOUR story. Nobody else can own it. It is yours. Hug it and Love it. Then when you're ready, share it, so you can help someone else.

5) There were days when Matt and I both wanted to run away and never come back. Sometimes I'd actually get a pit in my stomach as I would be returning from an errand and see my driveway ahead. But then I would remember what Peter said to Jesus in the Bible..." where would I go, Lord?" It was our faith–alone AND separately, that held us together. Faith was our glue. Find your glue. ASK for your glue to be shown to you. (See #1 again!) Your "glue" might come through a new friend or neighbor.

6) This may take a while and perhaps not even the following year or 3 afterward, but *eventually* do something special on your child's birthday and/or anniversary of passing. Commemorate, celebrate, and honor the special memories you shared with your child. Nobody can ever take those memories and experiences from you. Even on holidays, like Thanksgiving, which is my favorite of all, I make a little altar with pictures of ALL our loved ones who have passed on it. I keep it up for as long as I feel I have thanked and honored each one of those precious souls who have embellished my life. Be creative with your own rituals on your own holidays. Keeping their memory in your heart is a healthy thing to do. I love the word eventually. Break it down with me...**EVENT** (create an event/ritual) **U** (you get to do it) **ALLY** (the celebration will become your ally or friend!) The special rituals you create will bring you joy and invite your loved one's spirits into your sacred space, keeping their memory alive for you and for them. This will also allow you to pass on and share with other family members (your grandchildren especially) the gifts YOUR child or beloved contributed to your family tribe. Evan was a prankster and on April Fool's day, we always share the silly pranks he used to pull. We can laugh a lot about this now.

7) Lastly, practice gratitude for what you DO know and then be thankful for what you don't. We don't have to know everything, nor should we want to. Life is so full of mystery and surprises and you can be rest assured that GOOD will come out of ALL of our experiences. Not everybody will have *my* faith experiences or *my* healing discoveries. I'm

just sharing *my* story and maybe parts of it will be beneficial to you on some part of your journey. Use what you have been given. Each of us has been given a unique life. Start there. The willingness to start the journey of healing is the first step of the journey. Then watch for some surprising things to start unfolding. They will.

I've lost a parent, grandparents, and good friends to death. And now I've lost a child and it seems so different and unnatural than the other losses. I've yet to experience the death of a beloved pet, but any type of loss brings sadness including divorce. And it should, because love is such a powerful force that creates a void in our soul when we experience the loss of it. The cool thing about love is that it multiplies – just think how your life was before you had a partner, children, or any beloved pets. You still experienced love right? Love just multiplied and made room for more of it with whatever loving relationship you were graced with. Love grows in a relationship, and it doesn't stop growing when the subject of our affection goes back from whence it came... and somehow it can still keep multiplying. How do you say?

Cynthia Bourgeault is the author of a book that I highly recommend for anyone struggling with the death of a child or beloved. It is titled: <u>Love Is Stronger Than Death.</u> I stumbled upon this gem while I was in spiritual direction training in 2017-2018. In the forward of this book is written: Love between 2 people survives and becomes ever more truly itself **after** one of them dies. Love is most nearly itself when **here and now** cease to matter. (T.S. Eliot, "East Coker," V). The book pushes notions about life beyond death to an exciting new level...though at the time of death, it is *anything but exciting.*

I'll paraphrase what Cynthia means by this and what it meant for me. At the moment of our son's death, any petty nonsense abruptly stopped as well as any misunderstandings. I had to figure things out without him...but eventually, through a different kind of language, we met each other on a deeper level – without words. And forgiveness of any unfinished business was expressed in mystical and marvelous ways. Receiving a reiki healing session was just one example of how I experienced some healing through this new language and I will share with you later another message that Evan gave to me for his brother Mike which began with the clue of his boy scout neckerchief.

33

CHAPTER 5: SERVICES OR CELEBRATIONS OF LIFE

Planning a funeral is quite an educational experience especially when you are thrust into this planning without your head on straight.

I used to sing in the funeral choir at St. Joseph's Parish. I loved being able to serve the families who were honoring the life of their loved ones in this way. Music can be like a healing salve and old familiar hymns are like comfort food for the soul. I never thought a few years down the road we'd be the family sitting in the first pew. Choosing the songs for Evan's funeral was easier and more meaningful because I knew this group of caring people. I stood along-side them for many send-offs and now they were standing beside me. Their beautiful voices carried all the emotions swirling in that church and delivered them right to the altar of God. I was beyond appreciative of them and sharing their gifts of music. I think the music was the most memorable part of the entire ceremony. Evan loved music and I wanted it to be beautiful.

There is a process that takes place in the planning and preparing for a church funeral, or some other kind of memorial service and many people plan ahead when they know their departure time is nearing. Evan's accident was sudden, and we had no idea what to expect. One minute here, the next gone. Forever. We were told that Evan died immediately upon impact because the damage was so crushing, not only to his car but to his body. He had blunt-force trauma to the head, chest and limbs. The jaws of life had to come remove his body from his car. Matt and our son Mike know where the crash site happened. I was not interested in going to visit the scene. The attending officer drew on a piece of paper, the probable trajectory his car made before hitting the guard rail, crossing two lanes of oncoming traffic, spinning around, and then finally coming to a complete halt. There were 2 other cars involved in the accident. No-one else was killed and somehow that gave me some relief from the guilt that would have caused to all of us – especially Evan. I prayed and prayed for complete healing of all those involved in the accident – for years afterward –

until I sensed one day while sitting in a chapel, God telling me it was ok to stop now. We'll never know for certain, but it was suspected that Evan was driving too fast, lost control, and over-corrected which sent him into the guard rail, which spun him around, and in seconds it was all over.

I was told once by a medium, that Evan was reaching behind for something perhaps in the back seat and that's when he lost control. Both Matt and I believe this was very likely. When we were first teaching him to drive, we both noticed he could be inattentive at times. I guess the details don't really matter. Gone is gone.

I could envision the scene in my mind...but whenever Matt and I would drive to Madison after Evan's death, he would ask me if I wanted to see where the scene took place and my answer was always, "no."

A true story a few years ago, validated the scene as the officer had mapped out for Matt. In September of 2014 just 1 year after Evan's death, I was hired to be the part-time youth minister at St. Agnes Parish. Through my work there, I met many people from all over when we took high school teens on mission trips. Matt accompanied me one year on our trip to Detroit, Michigan. One of our connections made was with a couple around our age who had also lost a young adult son. Josh was also a musician and played in a band. Josh played drums, but Josh didn't die in a car accident. He had a heart condition from birth and died from circumstances around that.

We got to know Frank and Jan (and their son Aaron) and were invited to their home in Kalamazoo. In Winter. What happened on our drive home was almost unbelievable. The weather started turning bad as we were making the 6-hour ride back home. Rain turned to sleet and then to very heavy wet snow. Traffic on the 4-lane highway slowed to an absolute crawl. Matt was driving white-knuckled as the road was very slippery and I had my eyes peeled on the cars ahead making sure we had plenty of distance between us and them. We started seeing many vehicles slide into the ditch. All of a sudden a van came from behind us in the passing lane – driving the speed limit as if the weather was not an issue. It passed us and that's when the next several moments eerily played out before our eyes like a movie scene in slow motion. The back end of the van that just passed us started to fish-tail. The car ahead of us put on its brakes, forcing Matt to do the same...we both gasped as our tires were slipping and locking up. The speeding van then catapulted across the median to the opposite side of the highway – out of control-- now facing both lanes of the oncoming traffic before it somehow miraculously turned around. Not a single car was harmed in all of this split-second drama.

This terrifying scene took place in the blink of an eye. Matt and I both looked at each other in silence, having read each other's thoughts. After we caught our breath and traffic started *slowly* moving again, the weather started to let up. We continued driving cautiously and when we regained our normal breathing and composure I asked Matt if he thought that somehow we had just been shown the trajectory of what happened to Evan as he lost control of his car that night of the Blue Moon. Matt said he believed it 100%.

We had just spent the weekend with our new friends, consoling and reminiscing about our 2 sons and seeking answers each in our own way. I believed the officer's findings from the beginning, but now we both witnessed it together. It was a sobering moment. Our thoughts were united on it. We felt strangely privileged. It was de-ja-vu, like living a past experience in the present moment. The word that best describes it for me is "other-worldly."

After Matt had announced to our daughter Erin's family the news about Evan, he went back to work to shut off his computer and a co-worker/friend who had seen the police officer give Matt the "message to come home," asked Matt what happened and Matt told him. Brad put his hand on Matt's shoulder. Matt was crying and just said, "I have to leave now." From there he went to Newcomer's Funeral home.

We used their services 2 years prior when Matt's father passed away in 2010. He had a good experience with Newcomers back then and the comfort they offered drew him back there now. Matt is a task master. He notices when things need to get done and he takes care of them. This is one of his many gifts and one of the reasons I married him. So while I was at home making phone calls to family, he was taking care of other business. Matt's a good father, a devoted husband, and always goes the extra mile. He's a runner too, so that last part is literal as well as metaphorical. His dad taught him to "never quit." His natural effort to get the most important things done first is engrained in his character. Although he had been crying off and on all morning, up until this point he was keeping it together. He later told me he lost it and broke down when this young woman at Newcomers came over to ask if he needed help.

Megan was the gal's name and she listened to all Matt shared with her. He took her offer to help and later arranged to bring Evan's body to Green Bay from Madison and the next day our entire family went to Newcomers to make the funeral plans together. Megan was a young woman, maybe in her late twenties at best. She was from a small town in the Upper Penninsula of Michigan, (U.P.) like me, and she shared her personal story of losing her older sister in a car accident. Her story connected us. She had not planned a career working as a funeral home assistant but said losing her sister altered her career path. She was the perfect person to work with us. She knew my niece and played against their basketball team in high school. Another perfect connection. She helped us write Evan's obituary and worked with St. Joe's to set up services which were to be held the following Thursday, September 6th.

The biggest decision came next; Casket? Viewing? Cremation? How did we want this day to go? We decided on 1 day for everything. (In hindsight I wish we had done 2 days so we had more time to talk with friends of Evan's whom we did not know.) Everything happened so fast. I was thinking about Matt and the kids and what they wanted. I was worried about them more than myself. Megan asked how we felt about viewing the body. We decided easily on the cremation of his body, but she said that in sudden circumstances such as ours, it sometimes helps with closure if the family can see their loved one, one last time. Because of the autopsy, we already knew the damages to his body were extensive. Her voice reverberated compassion and she reassured us that she was extremely skilled at preparing loved ones for viewing. She said she would *honestly* let us know if she didn't think it was a good idea. We allowed her to give it a try.

The kids and Matt wanted to see Evan. I went along with whatever they wanted. It didn't matter to me, so I let them decide. Just our immediate family was able to see Evan. We picked out his clothes... a suit and tie...and she called us a couple of days later to come for a visit. She did a spectacular job. He looked so natural, so real, like he was just sleeping. No funny coloring or cakey make-up look. I gave Megan a crushed rose-petal rosary to put in his pocket, a gift given to me from Fr. Doug, a priest friend who had several years prior gotten it from a trip to Rome to see Pope John Paull II. I'll tell you; Megan was a great make-up artist. Not a mark on his precious head. And we were told not even one of his beautiful teeth had been chipped or broken. His orthodontist came to the funeral and I made sure to tell him that.

Evan looked peaceful. Matt and the kids were satisfied and I was glad for the decision they all made. I'm glad we got to be with Evan one last time together. Even though we chose cremation, we decided to have a casket for the funeral. His casket was closed on the day of the funeral, however. This special viewing was just for us. Megan let us know that the make-up only lasts in a controlled environment and only for a short time. We were grateful. I knew his spirit was already gone, that his body was now just a shell, but I ever so tenderly and gently brushed the coat sleeve of his suit, making one last caress of the one who's hand I used to hold in mine. Like a final sending-off until we meet again gesture.

The last time I saw Evan alive was 9 months earlier when he came home for Christmas of 2011. The memory I chose to hold onto was when he walked through our front door, dropped his bag and immediately came over to hug me and called me "Mama Bear."

After the viewing at Newcomers, Fr. Don came over to the house. We squared away all the business of the funeral, choosing the Scripture Readings, the songs, who would bring up the gifts of bread and wine, and if there would be a meal afterward. I think his words were relatable to Ann and Mike. He used the phrase "sitting in the shit" and that's not a word you hear priests say very often. But it described exactly what we were feeling at the time. He encouraged us to *feel those feelings.* Between church and the funeral home, all was taken care of for us. The meal after Mass was to be held downstairs in the church basement. We picked out flowers – a beautiful spray of white roses for the casket. All the plans fell together. We had some photo boards put together and my dear friend Anne, (the one who did the house blessing) made up some special bookmarks upon my request, that had a photo of Evan with a poem he wrote in 7th grade entitled, "I BELIEVE." I call it, "Evan's Creed" because it reflected the belief system of his heart.

One piece of advice I would give anyone going through this type of trauma is to: TAKE. YOUR. TIME. We have been conditioned to live in a fast-paced world and tie up loose ends quickly and neatly so we can get on with our busy schedules. Take the time _you need_ to process and plan, not the time that others think is appropriate. And plan the service, memorial, or celebration in the way you feel is right for you.

While it is true that some things need dealing with immediately, (like the physical, and bodily care of your beloved) it is _your_ life that has been turned upside down, and getting it done neatly in 1 day or 1 evening may or may not be the best option for you. In years past church funerals lasted 2-3 days for all the memories to be shared and people to come from far distances. And in some cultures, the memorials and services can last for a week or longer. Do what's right for you. Maybe a church funeral isn't what fits your needs. Matt and I had to make this decision together and at the time we did both agree that 1 day at our church would be best for us.

I've been to other types of services done right at the funeral home and 1 recently that was done outdoors on a Saturday with a Packer theme. This outdoor celebration was planned by my dear friend Donda, a mother who suddenly lost her 45-year-old son Jason. Jason loved the Packers and the outdoors and this celebration was a reflection of those things he loved in life with all of his best friends and family gathered around. One gift that was given was a tree to be planted in Jason's honor. Jason's family asked if the tree could be planted at our cabin on Blue Moon Lake.

Our cabin was given to us as a place to heal and now we are sharing it with another family as they heal. Our stories connect us even though the circumstances and details are different. And memorial services can be just as different. The traditional route is not better than a personalized, creative ceremony. At the core is the loss of a child and in our conditioned way of linear thinking, children aren't supposed to die before their parents. Funerals/Services can and should be tailored to honor the beloved's life with you as you are now sending them off on a new journey without you.

This is an act of courage on both sides because I truly believe in my heart, that their "essence" lives on. We now have to learn a new language of the heart. My experiences with Evan's spirit have convinced me of this. A ceremony of sending off is one of the most significant passageways that we all encounter at some point in our lives. They are the moments for most of us when heaven and earth meet when we are at our most vulnerable and OPEN to listening to the Divine. One door closes and another opens...but only our loved one is going through it.

One of the most important lessons I have learned from losing Evan is that the end of a physical body does not have to be the end of a relationship... unless you want it to be. Love Never Ends, means that love can continue to grow and offer healing even if that person is no longer here. The relationship can take on a new meaning and life of its own. My relationship with Evan has deepened beyond the loss of him physically. Spiritually we are connected and we have a special way of communicating now that is different and even better in some ways than before.

Another very important piece of advice is to allow each other to grieve and process at your own pace. Couples grow apart and together through all sorts of seasons in a marriage. But when a marriage is placed under what might be the most tremendous stress of all, it is essential to be able to grieve alone when needed and together when you are able. The grieving together is very very hard. All the little annoyances, resentments, and differences you have can be amplified. All kinds of old emotions come to the surface that are like a trap that is set, just waiting to divide you. This leads me to advice #3 (these are not in order of importance!)

For couples, find something that you can both cling to or agree upon. Our "something" was our faith in God, or what I now like to call The Divine. For a while, it may have been the only thread we were holding onto. But even *that* could turn into an argument. Our faith was challenged to the ultimate max. *How* we believed and *what* we believed in, *WITHIN our faith*, could be and was a source of contention. We both admitted there were times we wanted to go somewhere far away and never come back to face our new reality and deal with the aftermath of the seismic shock waves. Along with our faith in The Divine, was allowing others to surround and care for us. We needed solid friends to lean on. We were lucky and blessed to have them. It was an incredibly graced time to accept the offers for what it was we needed at each moment. Besides both having faith, we both had mutual respect for each other and that was also key in weathering our storm. We had been married 29 years at the time of Evan's death. This was not our first test or challenge, but it was where the "rubber met the road."

Seeking out professional and spiritual help as well as leaning on friends also became a necessity for us. When you experience such a devastating storm in life, it can take years of clean-up. The Compassionate Friends have chapters all over the world and there is a chapter in Green Bay that meets once a month. They are an international support group comprised of parents who have lost children. While I did not get too connected with this group, I did go to a few meetings with a friend who lost a daughter, and they were helpful. There are many people who have lost children and that common thread also offers a lifeline and an opportunity to meet new friends.

I sought out individual, professional counseling for myself, and eventually, that opened the door for other family members to seek counseling as well. One of the Deacons at our church also happened to be a family psychologist. I started meeting with him and he pointed me and our family to other helpful support groups and resources. The one tool I found most valuable *for me*, was the fact that at the time of Evan's death, I had been meeting with a spiritual director already for 10 years.

Spiritual Direction is when you sit with a trained individual and discuss any or all aspects of your life. A good spiritual director listens with the ear of the holy spirit and helps you discover for yourself, how God/The Divine is present in your life. They are not counselors and they do not give advice. They are trusted holy listeners who hold your sacred story as you reveal it to them in whatever way you need. Sister Caroline was my incredibly gifted spiritual director at the time. When she came to the funeral, she referred to Evan as Saint Evan. She was a God-send to me as I used to go to her retreat house (The Bridge Between in Cooperstown) when I needed the nurturing and silence offered there.

Although I have since changed my spiritual director, I'm 20 years in and have become a certified spiritual director myself since 2018. Continuing to be open and follow where the Spirit was guiding me, led me to some alternative healing resources as well which is how I started on the path to becoming a Healing Touch Practitioner. (More about that later!)

Thursday came. September 6, 2012, the day of Evan's funeral at St. Joseph Catholic Church. It was the grade school he attended and where he received his sacraments. Many times growing up he read the intercession prayers or

Scripture Readings from the podium on the altar during Mass. In 1st grade, he was one of the wise men for the Christmas play in church. As a family during Advent, we processed down the main aisle carrying a lit candle which we placed on the big wreath up front. We had many many good memories growing in our faith together as a young family there.

We had visitation at the church from 9 am-12:00 pm with the Mass starting at noon. Mass ended up starting late because there were SO many people who came. When the ceremony did begin, there was standing room only. All of our family and friends plus co-workers of both us and Evan filled the church. He had SO many friends From Green Bay, Oshkosh, and Madison. Evan had been working at Paison's in Madison, an Italian restaurant, and they all came. One father came on behalf of his son who had to work at Paison's that day. I suppose they had to have *some* staff.

The church was a little chaotic because of the sheer number of people that kept coming. I was a little perturbed about how Evan's casket was moved around to accommodate a better flow. First, it was positioned down by the altar, then they moved it to the front of the church where we were receiving people in line, then they moved it back in a little cove behind us. Did they think I would not notice this? Mothers have this instinctual sense when keeping track of their children. I suppose they kept moving him to make room for the hundreds of people coming through.

In hindsight maybe we should have considered a 2-day funeral, rather than trying to rush people through to keep to a timeline. We could have spent more quality time talking to people. Maybe the friend whose dad came in his place could have attended. Could have, should have. I'll have another side of guilt on my plate, please.

I wasn't mad at anybody in particular, (church, Newcomers staff, or God) but I think I may have just been feeling some low-level anger and I needed it to land somewhere. Those in charge were doing their jobs well. I'm still ever-grateful for all of them.

When the service finally did begin, Erin and I got up and said a few words. She shared a memory of Evan and then I shared a little Eucharistic message. The teacher in me wanted to take this opportunity and I felt compelled to say something. I said that even though Evan's body had been "taken and broken," it was also "blessed and given." These are words right from the Eucharistic prayer said by the priest at Mass. I whole-heartedly thanked all who came and invited them to share in communion with us. I made this invitation with intentionality because I wanted to make sure *everyone knew they were being invited to the table of our Lord who welcomes ALL. I suspected there were a lot of young people who were non-Catholics, but I didn't want anyone to feel left out. It was a very special day.*

I did not break down during Mass. I was still in shock and was holding it together. I could feel the love and support pouring out of people's hearts and into ours. The energy felt strong like a fortress holding me up. It was palpable. And although I wasn't counting, I think most everyone went up to receive communion. I did notice a few young people were not exactly sure how to receive the Host/Eucharist, but they just followed what others were doing and everything turned out fine. I think Evan was very proud of me for doing this. I was living up to my "Mama Bear" title with my courage to stand up at his funeral and bend the dogmatic rules just a little. Not 1 shred of guilt did I carry for this action. Who invites guests into their home and when it's time for dinner says, "This food I'm about to serve is only for some of you." This was the first time I found this separation of who can eat and who cannot eat at the table of our Lord very inadequate. So that is why I invited everyone to come up. I don't think this offended God in the least.

After communion at Mass, there is always that sacred silent time. Just like after eating a satisfying meal when all the dishes are done. I had asked my choir friend Gail to sing, "I Have Loved You With An Everlasting Love." I'll never forget the mixture of bitter-sweetness and depth her voice possessed as it covered the room like a velvet comforter. Tucking in all our broken hearts as we were "*seeking the face of God to bring us light and peace, his care and his love...calling us all by name and saying to us, You Are Mine.*" She has the voice of an opera singer.

It was the perfect song and the perfect singer. Everlasting Love. Eternal Love. Love that never ends. Love that cannot be taken away by death. In fact, death deepens it. It is still and always will be one of my favorite hymns. That moment was my most favorite part of the service. Music makes everything better. It resonates with the love language of the heart.

The rest of the Mass followed traditional protocol. There were the closing prayers, the sending-off song and final blessing (moment of truth), and then the procession out of the church. The pallbearers carried the casket outside as we followed behind. Then came the final separation. As the casket was given over to the staff at Newcomers to load into the back of the hearse and drive away. We were stationed on the sidewalk outside the church entrance to receive more hugs and comfort from friends. I kept looking over my shoulder to watch the vehicle carrying our son, pull slowly away. PAUSE.

We eventually went back into church to the basement where our catered meal was waiting to be served. TO EVERYONE. Our vulnerable spirits needed sustenance and nurturing on that special day and in that place. It was an occasion of coming together not dividing apart over who qualifies to eat a sacred meal. I think God is ok with my questioning it. My views on receiving Holy Communion are very different now after this experience. It doesn't feel wrong. It feels more expansive and inclusive.

The chicken dinner was delicious and physically nourishing and gave us more time to be together. We were able to talk with more people and it felt relaxed. All in all, the day did not feel much like a celebration to me because it felt incomplete.

It felt rushed and I think Evan's amazing friends probably had some good stories to share that would've been wonderful for us to hear. To have a 3-hour visitation and then a 1-hour Mass was not nearly enough time. Even with the added mealtime afterward, 1 day was still not enough time to properly honor and celebrate Evan's life. A few close friends and neighbors did come to our home afterward as well as family who helped put all the food away and continue to take care of us the rest of the day. Another gratitude.

Well, Evan, Here I am 11 years later and with this book, I am celebrating and honoring your life! I think now I feel more satisfied that this job is coming nearer to completion. I hope you feel the same. I LOVE YOU!!! TO THE MOON AND BACK!

The funeral planning and the actual funeral were a lot to process in just 5 days. Even though perhaps I would have done some things slightly differently, I was and always will be grateful to our church community, Newcomers, and everyone who helped in the slightest way. We had so many meals given to us, both homemade, frozen, and gift cards. We were taken care of for months afterward. Our blessings were too numerous to count.

I guess upon further reflection, everything turned out just perfect. It is OUR story, and it is a beautiful story. It was a week frozen in time. I threw out the dress I wore that day. I did not want to wear it ever again. It served the purpose for that day only. I guess that was a good sign that I wanted to move forward from that day as I was already choosing to focus on the good.

Processing the death of a child or beloved will be unique for each person. Being good and patient with yourself is key. I thought I was those things, but I learned a whole new level of self-care during my 11-year journey after the death of our son. Try surrounding yourself with trusted family, friends, professionals, and trained support.

Follow your intuition and don't be afraid to ask questions. God designed us to be curious co-creators. Be with the folks that are courageous enough to "sit in the shit" with you on the ugliest, dark days of your grief. Life is going to be difficult for a while and different forever. New people will probably come into your life – like shining stars who will help give you hope and shed some light on your path. Accept help, especially around any holiday or anniversary, especially the first year, and maybe for a longer time if need be. Just don't stay there too long...others are needing your gifts to the world.

Even though I withdrew almost completely for a few months afterward, some people kept reaching out and that is what helped the most. They were my courageous friends and acquaintances that were not afraid to enter my space of sitting in darkness and gloom. We wanted to talk about Evan. I loved when friends would ask me to share things about him. People kept caring and caring and caring and they didn't stop caring. People who have lost children are some of the best caring people I have ever met. *I want to be one of those caring people for YOU.* One of Matt's co-workers sent us a card on every holiday and Evan's birth and death anniversary – for 2 years! Becky Bond – you have no idea how healing and loving those cards were. THANK YOU! Just know that there are lots of people out there who are waiting to throw you a buoy or life-jacket and want to just love on you and wait with you while you are processing your heaviest of grief. There will be many good surprises that come your way along this journey...and your mourning WILL turn to dancing... if you accept the invitation. I promise.

CHAPTER 6: OUR SON

Being Evan's mother was an honor and privilege. Evan was my firstborn child and his life changed mine forever. When Matt & I got married, I didn't want any children of my own. My parents had recently divorced and remarried, enlarging our core family with 7 other children. I could see by observing and interacting with them that blending families was very difficult so we took our time with expanding our family. Matt and I had a ready-made family with his daughter Erin from a previous marriage. I was happy with that arrangement and we got along well with Erin's mom. But that sweet little blond-haired Erin may have influenced my desire to have children over time. Watching her and Matt interact with each other was joyful. She used to ride her bike alongside him when he went running. She was always telling her little friends how pretty I was. She stole my heart from day 1.

There were SO many joy-filled memories of Evan, watching him and Michael James throw leaves and helicopters in the Fall air just to have them float gently down and do it again and again. Or the time I watched them "paint" the weathered wooden fence that bordered our neighbor's yard. I gave them each a paintbrush and a bucket of plain old water. The water made the wood "appear" darker, but then it would dry about 10 minutes later…so they would have to go back and "touch it up."

When Evan was about 4, he would kneel or stand on a kitchen chair and help me bake cookies. We did this a lot because I love to bake. But one of my all-time favorite memories of Evan was in summer when he was about 6 years old. I had given the kids sidewalk chalk and they were creating all sorts of artwork on the concrete. I was working in the yard and at one point I walked by Evan – he lifted up his head and looked directly at me – he had taken the white chalk and colored his entire face with it! He looked like a little pantomime, grinning from ear to ear. I quickly grabbed my camera (this was before cell phones!) and snapped a photo. I never knew what crazy, funny things he would do! We had a video recorder, and he would always ask me if he could look through the camera lens. He was always so curious and full of wonder. Always so inquisitive and wanted to know how things worked.

And he was very very smart. I don't think I realized just how smart he was until in high school he built his own computer and created 2 hard drives on it. He was a straight-A student and didn't have to work very hard to get good grades. He did like to pull harmless pranks and he had a dry sense of humor. One time we had friends coming over for dinner and he taped the handle down on the water sprayer on the sink so when I turned on the water to do dishes, it squirted me! He also did this same little trick when he worked in the lab with his dad at Bay Valley Foods in the summers.

One of his most infamous tricks however was (and I didn't get to witness this) he somehow was able to hook up a universal remote to the tv in the high school cafeteria and was able to change the channel at will. I don't think he ever got caught. Anyway – he was very technologically gifted and always curious about how things worked. And he was very organized. *He liked to categorize things and keep lists.* I would ask him for a Christmas list and one year, even though there was not much on the list, he had researched each item and had columns listed of where you could purchase the item and the cost. I guess he wanted to make our shopping for him easier. I still laugh about this!

Evan was not very materialistic. He lived very simply as a young adult and was into thrifting and 2nd hand stores. He could stretch a dollar so that he could spend more of his money on playing music and his recording equipment which I think he contemplated turning into a career. That was most important to him. And having fun with friends.

The day after the accident, we drove to Madison and picked up all his things in 1 trip. He didn't have much. The last place he lived was an old house that he shared with about 5 or 6 other guys. That fall he decided to go back to school at MATC and was taking classes that had nothing to do with music. It seemed to us that he was making a transformation and rethinking his career path and perhaps his life path. He was also wrestling with his beliefs. He shared with Matt that he wasn't sure he believed in God anymore. This alone shows me the courage and trust he had in being able to talk to his dad about such a monumental issue. I know Matt handled the conversation much better than I would have at the time.

The classes Evan started that fall were geared toward the modern sciences. Among those courses were Biochemistry Engineering and Quantum Physics, a total turnaround from the music world. In the most basic definition, Quantum Physics is the science of possibilities, where *everything exists simultaneously outside of space and time.* There is no space/time continuum in the quantum realm of possibilities, there is only *pure potential* of those possibilities.

When I found out he was taking these classes I was really curious why he was all of a sudden interested in a change of direction. I never had a chance to talk with him about it. With the announcement to his dad about doubting if there was a God, and these new classes he was taking, it seemed like he was searching for a deeper meaning to life. I can't say for sure, but it seemed that way. A few years later I went through his book bag which had some old mail and other papers stuffed into it. I thought it was time to go through and see if there was anything important to hang onto. As I was making a pile for trash, an old paystub envelope flipped over *and I noticed a list on it, written in red ink in his handwriting.*

I stopped what I was doing and just stared at the envelope and the mysterious items he had listed. There were 5 items on it, and it appeared to me that these were things that he wanted to research when he had time. They were:

1. *Pandora's Box* – Alexander Christopher
2. *The Pleiadian Mission* – Randolph Winters
3. *Sourcefield Investigation* – David Wilcock
4. *Journey of Souls* – Michael Newton
5. Edgar Cayce

I was rather bewildered as I gazed at these items. For weeks it felt like I was being "nudged" to go through the chest where I had Evan's papers stored. It felt like he had just left me some breadcrumbs to follow up on because I had recently purchased and read the life of Edgar Cayce. The book "called out" to me as I was shopping in Barnes & Noble one day. I was fascinated by Edgar's life story as being known as the sleeping prophet who would go into a trance and give detailed instructions for healing people of all kinds of diseases and chronic illnesses. I looked up all the other items on the list and found things like "remote viewing," "past life regression," ESP, and some alleged conspiracy theories. Hmmm. I saved the envelope.

When I looked up *Pandora's Box*, by Alexander Christopher, I found that it was a book that was updated in 2007 and described as, "the Ultimate Unseen Hand" behind the agenda of the New World Order.

In it, Christopher exposes the players behind the globalist agenda, what they have done in the past, what their plans are for the future (are we there yet?), and some of the underpinnings of control factors in Western society. Apparently, this book must have contained some important information because the CIA is said to have raided the author's house. I tried to order the book, but it's not available anywhere, not even on Amazon. (You can download a pdf version of it on the internet but you can find a lot of stuff on the internet that is not true.) In its 620 pages, it has some pretty crazy chapters like, "The Origin of Misinformation," "The True Story of the Federal Reserve," "The John F. Kennedy Assassination," and "The Plan to Starve the American People."

Doesn't sound too far-fetched to me if you're paying attention to what's happening today. Evan did a report in high school on Area 51 and aliens. I think he had a burning desire to know the truth about a lot of things. I was starting to wonder if he was trying to tell us that we should pay attention to some of these things.

After Evan's death, I read lots of books about the afterlife. I found on Evan's Facebook page that his favorite movie was "What The Bleep Do We Know," so I tracked down a copy and watched it. That movie was the first time I'd heard anything explaining about quantum physics. It opened my eyes to explore a whole new world. What really blew me away was when I went in for my initial interview with the Spiritual Guidance Training Program (SGTP) at Siena, and I found that movie in their bookstore.

I gradually became more interested in energy healing not only because of my reiki experience, but it seemed a whole new expansive world was being opened to me. And who are the Pleiadians? In one of my healing touch training classes, we were allowed to choose 1 book from many that were displayed on 2 large tables and I happened to notice one entitled: *The Pleiadian Promise*, by Christine Day. Of course, I snatched it up! In her book, Christine explains that self-love opens a great potential within us to carry a depth of compassion and empathy for other human beings and if we can receive the frequency of unconditional love, we can live free from fear and come back into an authentic alignment to our sacredness as human beings. She also states as multi-dimensional beings who are evolving, we will have no need for ego which causes separation and competition, and together we will form a collective union of trust based on truth from within[1].

I'm not sure what exactly to think about all that...I'm just laying it out there because of that little envelope that was left behind in Evan's book bag and the experiences I started having on my journey. Sounds to me like a lot of changes in our world about truth and our ability to heal ourselves. One thing for sure is how I feel in my heart...and I feel that all of this is Evan's legacy not only to me but to the world. Truth, Love, and Healing. And Peace.

He has helped me AWAKEN and open my mind to other possibilities and potential truths that await us as we move forward in our evolution. And he has helped me to move away from my stuckness and judgmental ways of thinking. The cracks in my broken heart were making more room for the expansive love and healing awaiting me. I look at Evan's death a whole lot differently today. To get to a point where I can honestly say "thank you" for the gift of your life Evan.... *and thank you, for the gift of all that your death has taught me. This takes honor and celebration of a life lived to a whole new level. I'm so proud to have been your mother. Thank you for teaching me.*

In 2017 while in training at St. Catherine of Siena, I came across another book by Cynthia Bourgeault that seemed to be tilted out towards the edge of the bookshelf as if it was beckoning me to read it. It was. The book was *The Meaning of Mary Magdalene, Discovering the Woman at the Heart of Christianity.* On page 167 it states, (according to Ms. Bourgeault's theory), that the resurrection of Jesus was not something that happened only once to Jesus, but is the living reality and meeting ground *of all* who have traveled to the endpoint with a beloved and discovered that **"the object of their affection has become the subject of their truth,"** *the very matrix in which they now swim.*

---

[1] Day, Christine, Brandon, Jodi; *The Pleiadian Promise*, Weiser; First Edition (April 17, 2017) pg 115.

Stay with me here now as I try my best to explain this statement. Love makes an alchemical transformation (literally) when people love each other the way Jesus showed us to love. Whether the relationship is between parent and child, husband and wife, or 2 close friends makes no difference. *Divine Love creates a unifying bond.* So to use my personal life example, my son Evan was the "object" (the person who affected my life) of my affection and became the "subject" (cause) of my truth. I believe with my whole heart that I am carrying out his legacy in the writing of this book.

I knew absolutely NOTHING about physics much less quantum physics and the relationship it has with healing. The Bible also teaches that Jesus is still alive through the workings of the Holy Spirit, and in the book *The Cloud of Unknowing,* author unknown, it says, *"My soul lives where it loves."* Somehow this makes sense to me, and I believe the essence of Evan's spirit lives on in the love we carry of him within us. If it's true for me and my loved one, then it's true for you. I think it's a collective love essence.

Working through my own healing journey and discovering this has given me much comfort. And not only comfort, but *confidence in knowing the resurrection experience became real for me.* Not only with Jesus (who I love and is my BFF, just ask my kids!) but also with Evan. That is why I not only thrive after losing Evan but am joyful beyond what I ever thought possible. His spirit is alive and No-one can steal my joy. After his resurrection, Jesus came back and appeared to his disciples and gave them some parting instructions...our loved ones can do this too. Evan has done this with me and other family members and most likely some of his friends. We just have to be open to the new language of our other senses to receive the messages they are trying to send us.

The story of Jesus didn't just happen two thousand plus years ago, and yet it did according to Ms. Bourgeault. Although I am NOT a bible scholar or theologian, I have completely read and studied the bible probably more than the average person. I have taken college courses in both the Old and New testaments and am always studying in bible classes along with reading the daily scriptures for many many years. God gifted me with an incredibly curious mind, to observe and critically think so I can observe things from many angles – not just the bible and what religion has taught us. In spiritual direction training, we learned a lot about our biases and are taught to look at things from many different perspectives as we listen to other's stories.

Since Evan's death 11 years ago, something changed in me and the way I read and ponder what Jesus might have been trying to teach his disciples. Somewhere around 2010, the following verse became a lamppost for me and continues to light my path to this day. It is John 14:12. This account from the Gospel of John shares what Jesus said to his disciples when he appeared to them after the resurrection. "Very truly, I tell you, the one who believes in me will also do the works that I do and in fact, will do *greater works than these,* because I am going to my Father.[2]"

Through my new expanded, yet basic understanding of quantum physics (of which I am no expert either) together with my experiences of death, loss, spiritual guidance, and alternative healing, those words came alive to me in a new way. It seemed at least to me, that there was much more Jesus was trying to tell them *and us...about how we are to live in the now! Do you think it's possible that Jesus could be telling us that AS we believe and step into our divinity, we help bring Heaven to Earth? Or in other words, was he trying to explain that we don't have to wait until we die to ascend to Greatness?*

Maybe this is what's meant by Ms. Bourgeault about pushing current notions about life-beyond death to an exciting new level. Could it be possible that God, as the Author of life, sent Jesus to show us he was passing on that authority and also telling us that **we** have the power to heal and transform ourselves and the world as well? If we too are made in the image and likeness of God, doesn't it make sense that our full potential could also be this intermingling of our humanity and our divinity to live more fully ON earth AS IT IS in Heaven? I now have more questions than answers, but this makes sense to me.

When I tossed *The Family God Uses* into the trash and started believing in the lie that God couldn't possibly use *my* family, I started falling down a deep dark hole. This accelerated with Evan's death.

I didn't cry at Evan's funeral. I may have teared up a few times, but I didn't cry. I was more concerned about others who were upset and I wanted them to be ok, especially my nephew Scott who was a year older than Evan and whose birthday was the same day as Evan's accident – September 1st. I know now that the state of shock I was in, was like a protective barrier surrounding me. When Scott approached me, we hugged and I told him that he now has a very special angel watching over him from Heaven.

---

[2] New Revised Standard Version (NRSV) Bible: Anglicised Catholic Edition

In the months that followed the funeral, I moved from shock into a deep depression. I became clinically depressed and had to go on medication to function on some level. I began to discover lies, betrayals, and dysfunction that came to the surface and into my awareness. I was trying to understand and process these things as they came up. I was also trying to understand who were the people I could most trust to help me through this crisis. I had to figure out what this absolutely life-altering devastation was trying to teach me about myself and how I was to move forward in life. I won't say "move on," because you don't leave something of this magnitude behind you. You carry it "with" you. Forever. It forever changes who you are.

I'm so grateful now for that lesson. I was not looking to blame anybody except maybe myself...and that's what took me down the rabbit hole of depression. I was listening to the "lies" telling me I wasn't a good enough mother. For a while I started to believe if I had been more this way or that way...this whole crisis could have been avoided. I felt surrounded, like Noah in the ark, surrounded by vast seas and turbulent storms tossing and crashing up against the boat on every side. I remember one day, at my lowest point, looking at our medicine cabinet and opening it up. I thought how simple and easy it would be to just swallow a bunch of pills and never wake up. It was a fleeting moment, but it really happened. I wasn't thinking in my right mind.

I love snow globes – even the cheap little ones. I love shaking them up and watching the snow fall gently back into place. But now I felt like I was trapped inside of one, suspended in the air and I couldn't find my grounding. I was not in control of where I might land.

I remember going to the chapel in Champion, WI, better known as the Shrine of Our Lady of Good Help, to kneel in front of the statue of Mary in the downstairs crypt. I would stare into young Mother Mary's eyes and beg for tears to come. When I looked into her face, her eyes would meet mine. No words needed to be spoken between us. She had lost a son too. She knew how I felt. Yet no tears came. Then one morning, close to the 1-year anniversary of Evan's death, I experienced what must have been a miraculous healing. I woke up and walked into our kitchen and as I did, it felt like a light switch had been flipped. I felt a subtle shift and I felt lighter inside like something had been instantly lifted off of me. Within 2 weeks I stopped taking the anti-depressant

I was on and little by little the numbness made way gradually for me to start feeling my feelings without being overwhelmed all at once. There were still no tears, but I was slowly starting to feel alive again. It was like the novocaine was wearing off.

The story about the chapel in Champion is from 1859 when a young Belgian girl named Adele Brice had a vision of Mary as she was walking through the woods. A crypt was built and then a Shrine, but it was on December 8, 2010, that the Shrine was declared an official Marion Shrine due to many proven miracles that took place there. The Shrine, just 20 minutes outside of Green Bay now ranks with places like Our Lady of Lourdes in France and many other well-known places throughout the world where there have been sightings of Mary and thousands of miracles.

When our daughter Ann was in high school after the boys graduated, I would sometimes drop her off at school and head to the Shrine to pray for her through Adele's intercession. Ann, like Evan, had also decided she was not going to receive the sacrament of Confirmation in 11th grade. Adele was told by Mother Mary that she was to build a school out in this wild country and teach the children about Jesus. I thought Adele could help me out – or at least listen to my mother's heart about me also wanting my children to know Jesus. I kept this all to myself.

On her 16th birthday, I took Ann horseback riding at Kurtz Corral in Door County. On our way home she mentioned to me out of the blue, that she knew I was disappointed about her not getting confirmed, but she didn't want to do something "just because everyone was doing it." She explained to me that it had to mean something to her. She did say, however, (and I have to tongue-in-cheek tell you this) that if she ever DID get confirmed, she would choose the name "Adele" for her confirmation name. I NEVER TOLD ANN ABOUT THE PRAYERS I HAD ASKED OF ADELE BRICE.

Ann is still not confirmed today, but I never put limits or time frames around miracles or how God intends to move hearts. I pulled out my Adele Brice prayer card again lately. I've been asking for her help again because Ann shared with me that she was struggling with the 10-year anniversary of her brother's death. Our daughter Ann is a rebel. God has big plans for her. And she does love Jesus.

There were so many ups and downs and stages of grief. I was grieving losses *before* Evan's death. I was so worried about my children being overcome by the culture. Now with Evan gone, I don't worry about him anymore. I feel at peace knowing that somehow he is helping us. Death doesn't scare me so much. It isn't the end of our love. I have chosen to carry Evan with me in my heart as I move forward in my life. It was BECAUSE of his earthly presence and the love we shared, that my mission in life has been AFFECTED and alchemically altered. I say alchemical because there really was a transformation – a transformative change not only in him bodily but in my essence too. After his death, the resurrection (life after death) story became our story too. It was a lived experience or what I call the John 14:12 experience.

Hope

Life really is a mystery and each day is a precious gift. The ordinary days are the binding glue of our stories.

I have referred to this book a few times in my story. *The Family God Uses, Leaving a Legacy of Influences* by Tom & Kim Blackaby. I mentioned in Chapter 3 that I re-shelved it, but at my lowest point, I took it off the shelf and actually threw it in the trash. I didn't believe God would use what I considered at the time, a "messed up family like mine." Unlike the family in the book, I felt our family was not heading towards a happily ever after ending. As a young family, we HAD been involved in many community service activities through our church and school. We DID pray as a family. I started losing hope because I felt the outside world was having more of an influence on our teenagers than we as parents did. I felt like I was a failure of a mother. I started to doubt everything and trust nothing, yet I clung to my faith and kept digging deeper to try and understand the meaning of where I was being led.

In hindsight, I can see the meaning was to discover the deeper roots of my faith. I recognized back then that we were heading for trouble as a family – and I could have abandoned my faith, but I stayed in the boat while the sea was raging all around us. A good friend of mine, Connie, once sent me a card of encouragement, knowing I was going through rough times. She said something to the effect, "Sometimes God calms the storm...and sometimes he lets the storm rage as he calms the child." I never forgot that.

Different and alternative ways to find healing began opening up for me and while I was skeptical, all of them were weighed and tested against the backdrop of my catholic roots. The most basic of these healings was to believe beyond a doubt that I was created by love, for love, to love – MYSELF first – so that I could love others well. My relationship with myself, that I was worthy and good enough, seemed to be the message Mary was sending me in our "heart to heart" meetings in the crypt at the Shrine. I don't know how it happened exactly, but I believe in my heart my clinical depression was healed miraculously through Mary. I was always preaching to others to love themselves, but I wasn't loving myself very well. I had to learn how to practice what I preached and be good to myself and not believe this lie that I wasn't good enough. Going through the 2-year spiritual guidance program was immensely healing and opened my eyes more fully to see that I was not honoring my own story the way God saw my story.

I learned to love my imperfect self. I was imperfectly perfect in God's eyes... and I came to know this in my heart. I am forever grateful to the staff at Siena for this experience. On the front of my brochure for spiritual direction, I have a quote from the poet Ralph Waldo Emerson that says, "The unexamined life is not worth living. [3]" And another much simpler quote is "Know Thyself." The latter quote goes back to the ancient Greek philosophers, Socrates and Plato, and was inscribed on their temple entrances.

No matter how death comes, it seems to me when we experience the loss of a child, we are left with many questions. I was forced to reflect on my relationship with others, including Evan, and ultimately with myself and the Divine within myself.

On July 18, 2022, two days from what would have been Evan's 34th birthday, I was rummaging through some of his personal papers (again) to do some research for this book and I found some cards I had sent him in the mail while he lived in Madison. He had saved them. I'll say that again because it makes me feel good. *He had saved them* and after his death, his best friend Breezi discovered a box with these personal items in them and made sure we got them. I found the last birthday card we sent him which was postmarked on July 19, 2012. On the cover of the card, it said:

[3] Emerson, Ralph Waldo, "Self-Reliance," 1841.

(Italics included)

Dear Son,

Ever since you were born, I *worried and wondered* about whether or not I was being the *best parent* I could. Did I make you *feel important?* Did we find enough time for the little things – like *laughter and hugs, and "just-between-us" moments?* And, even when we disagreed, did you always know I loved you?

(On the inside)

Of all the things I've done in my life, one thing I'd *never change* is *having you for a son...*If I didn't say it, I hope I always showed it – I'm *proud* to be your parent, and *I love you, Son.*

Happy Birthday

Love,

Mom & Dad

(Inside the card I had inserted a small prayer card. It was that same picture of Jesus that was framed above our sofa in the living room.)

Even the fact that Evan saved these cards, as small as that is, means something to me now. He didn't throw them away.

Life is a mystery and it is a beautiful thing to have had the gift of Evan. Even if it was for a short time. The details around his death don't matter to me. The things that happened don't take away from the fact that I am, we were, and still are, proud to have been his parents.

On July 14, 2022, I found out about another family very close to ours, lost their oldest son Jason, suddenly and without warning at the age of 46. I just wonder if we'll be able to share some comfort and healing with them because of our membership in "the club." It feels raw like gold being tested in the fire. Again.

Here I am Lord. Use me.

I received a text from this mother a few days later on the 19th, saying: "How did you get through the pain?" I called her immediately and we spoke for a while about the details of her son's death and how she was making plans to have a *celebration of life* in a couple of months. She shared with me a profound moment of peace that overcame her after she had been sobbing for a long time. She was crying and she told her son that "she just wanted him to come home with her." She shared that all of a sudden, a feeling of peace came over her as she heard his voice say that he **was** coming home with her. She said this peace was overwhelmingly calming and she stopped crying. I told her I believed she did indeed hear his voice, and to trust it. **He was coming home in her heart where God already resides within. They will be together in that sacred space forever because "Home" is where the heart is and where the Divine dwells.**

Looking back over the 10 years since Evan's passing, HOPE — this concept of things unseen — manifested into real things, seen. I could "see now through a different way of looking." Some refer to this as seeing with the eyes of your heart. Hope only becomes real when you experience it manifesting in your life. It's like that glue I talked about. It's what you cling to **while you are waiting** for the deeper meaning of what it feels like when "*Your mourning will be turned into dancing* or *Your tears will turn into Joy*." It might be helpful to remember that Jesus said many times, "Your FAITH healed you." He didn't say "Your religion healed you."

These are just some of the things that became manifest in my experience through hope.

- Openness — an expansive, deepening of my faith and intimacy of the Divine within
- Healing on many levels in myself and our entire family using various methods of energy healing that have helped each of us in our own way and at our own speed. (Reiki/Healing Touch/ Ancestral- Shamanic Healing, etc)
- Reconciling the conflict that came up for me between using alternative healing and my faith. (Still working on this!)
- Growth in my Self-Care, accepting ALL the imperfect aspects of myself that needed loving

- Development of a renewed strength and emboldened spirit in speaking my truth
- Sharing my miracles of healing and letting others know that the same is available for you.

My greatest hope and joy would be to journey with you *in the waiting,* you who have lost a child, so you too may experience this transformative reality that your beloved is truly closer than you think and never leaves you. And to feel changed from the inside out as you look at life from a new perspective. "Behold, I make ALL things new again." (Rev 21:5)

CHAPTER 7: FRAGMENTATION OF THE FAMILY UNIT

Evan's death was the catalyst that started to dismantle a lot of what was NOT working for us in our family. Looking back, it seems like a major pruning took place. All the dead branches that were not bearing fruit were cut, in order that we would grow stronger as a family unit.

After being off from work at NWTC for 2 full weeks, I went back and worked for 2 weeks before I quit working altogether. On those days when I did work, I would come home and lie on the couch and zone out in front of the television until it was time for bed. I was basically existing and numb. We were all grieving in different ways and trying to cope the best we could. Matt went back to work which I know was not easy for him either and Ann and Mike were struggling too. They were blindsided by their brother's death. I was not there for them in their pain – I was "checked out" as their mother.

I was sinking into a deep depression and when I came home from work one day, a foundational boundary had been crossed by our 2 young adult kids which resulted in both of them leaving. They found other places to stay while trying to sort things out. I had to explain to Matt when he came home, what happened and why they left. He was not happy with me. Every day it was getting harder and harder to get out of bed. Instead of having lost 1 child, it felt like we had lost 3. My thoughts were..."What is happening here?" My life was falling apart right before my eyes. I couldn't have felt any lower. I had no way of knowing what they were going through and how they were processing their trauma, but I clearly knew that their ways of dealing with it ***at that time*** were not in the highest good of our family. I risked them not loving me by upholding boundaries that protected our sacred ground we called "home," and I let them go out the door.

I did not ask where they were going. They each packed a bag and left quietly and respectfully. I risked them not loving me and that was harder than losing a child who did. So now everybody was upset. It was a very lonely time. EVERYTHING we instilled in our children – all the things we believed in, invested in...foundational faith values, moral integrity, love, and respect – as humanly flawed as we modeled them – were now being tested to the max. Was I going to be a coward and try to be their "friend," or was I going to be their parent who was upholding good values? This was the hardest thing I have ever done as a human being and a parent, *especially* after having just dealt with the loss of Evan.

With a "mama bear" attitude, a boldness rose up inside of me to fight the influencing culture that was trying to weaken our family bonds. It was a spiritual battle, attacking when we were at our weakest point. It was for me the defining moment as a parent of young adults who were looking for ways, in my opinion, that would only temporarily ease their pain. It was tough love and it was a lesson I came to master.

Some say that our children are our best teachers. I can now say with a sincere heart, *Thank you God for my children and the lessons I have learned from them.* I would rely on and repeat often this ancient wisdom of Scripture from Thessalonians 5: 16-18, "Rejoice evermore. Pray without ceasing. In EVERYTHING give thanks, for this is the will of God in Christ Jesus *concerning you.*" I would start writing my own prayers and this one I called "The Scary Mom's Prayer." It was included in an article about our Blue Moon experience and Evan's death. It was published in our diocesan newspaper, The Compass on 9/14/14.

"Thank you, God for the gift of Your children.

Lord, they are not mine, they are Yours.

If they are doing something that's hurting them,

Stop them in their tracks."

After Evan's accident...I'd read that prayer and had this fear come over me, that I better be darn careful what I'm asking for.

Now with all 3 young adults gone, I not only quit my job, but I also quit being a volunteer catechist for 9th-grade religious education classes. I shut down almost completely. What could I possibly teach kids now about their faith – when mine was on the verge of collapse? I also quit the Religious Studies Program I was enrolled in at Silver Lake College. I felt I was a complete and utter failure as a mother and teacher. What business did *I* have, trying to impact young people when my own family life was in shambles?

The Religious Education Director at that time was Tina Meyers and she tried to encourage me in October of 2012 to come back to teach, but I returned all my teaching books and even some of my own materials for my replacement to use. I was swallowed up in my "dark night of the soul." I couldn't see or feel God, only darkness. Tina didn't give up, however, and she called me again in December and persuaded me to come back in January. I did. Somehow, by the grace of God, I was able to go back into the classroom with my 9th-grade teens. And Matt came with me. My rock, my support my "catholic bouncer." I'm forever grateful to Tina for encouraging me and convincing me to come back and teach. I'm forever grateful for having such a supportive husband whom I consider my best friend. I had to walk into the pain and fear and not try to avoid or go around it, which would only end up prolonging it. I had to face it head-on.

I was beginning to see glimmers of light here and there. In time, I eventually went back to my studies at Silver Lake and finished in 2015 with a certification in Religious Studies with an emphasis on youth ministry. It took me a lot longer to achieve that goal, but all things considered, I finished and finally crossed the goal line. Along with Matt, our friends Rick and Sandy Detry were there to help honor this huge milestone with me.

I continued my journey with a youth ministry apprenticeship at St. Joe's and then another attack on my faith and another sign from God came through to show me, I was not alone. More doubt started creeping in before being hired as youth minister at St. Agnes Parish where I worked from 2014-2017. Midstream through the apprenticeship, I started doubting my abilities to connect with and be a mentor to teenagers. I remember the day clearly. I had minor surgery on my foot and was driving down Oneida Street towards home. I was *having a conversation in my head with God, telling Him I was "too old" to* be a youth minister! "I'm 52 years old for God's sake. What teens are going to listen to someone my age? What do *I* have to offer?" God must have been rolling his eyes at my whining. Suddenly, a car pulled up next to me, passed by, and pulled directly ahead of me into my lane. The license plate on that car read: **APLAN4U.** Well...I know this was a Scripture verse from Jeremiah 29:11, "For I know the plans I have for you, plans to bring you prosperity and not disaster, *plans to bring about the future you hoped for."* The Divine knew how to get my attention. The message was real and resonated inside of me.

Jeremiah is known as the "weeping prophet" who was always complaining to God that he was "too young." After I received this message, I did a quick reality check and stopped the whining that I was "too old," and decided to trust in a bigger plan. With gratitude.

Matt and I took one day, one step at a time during these years when we were trying to regain our footing. We stayed connected and tried reaching out to help Ann and Mike the best we could. They both came back home, they both left again...and again and we just kept trying to support them while we were trying to keep ourselves afloat. We kept moving forward in our own personal healing journeys and AS we were able to strengthen ourselves little by little, we were able to let that strength uphold them. Our foundation needed a lot of "shoring up" but we never *ever* gave up. It seemed the right people just kept coming alongside us on each leg of the journey. We both are so grateful. That's not to say we didn't have lots of twists and turns, ups and downs on our path. Life does not seem to get easier. It just seems that we have been able to react differently now and we have come a very long way in communicating better as a family.

Just like a marriage relationship continues to need work, so do all the members of a family need continual work and maintenance. We are still to this day continuing to do our inner work as individuals. Matt and I as the elders of the family have made doing this work from the inside out <u>a priority</u>. In order to make an effective change that radiates outward, we took a good long hard look inside ourselves and then took action to make the changes we desired to extend to our family. It has been very hard work, and SO worth it. But we still have not "arrived." Remember those loose ends I talked about earlier? We are still learning and growing and forgiving and accepting where each of us is. There are still times of chaos when raw feelings or loose ends come to the surface in need of some attention, but we have not given up. And our foundation has been incredibly fortified and strengthened. Our family has increased in number and we still count those on the "other side" in that number. (Oh when the saints go marching in!) And most of all, our trust in God, whether the size of a mustard seed or mountain, is what holds us together. I can now definitely relate to chapter 11 of Hebrews in the Bible. The story of how our ancestor's faith overcame seemingly insurmountable obstacles. From Cain and Abel to Noah, from Sarah and Abraham, Isaac, Jacob, Moses, Rehab, and all the Israelites crossing the Red Sea…it was their FAITH that sustained them. Ecclesiastes 4:12 says: "Two people can resist an attack that would defeat one person alone. But a rope made of 3 chords is not easily broken." It is faith that strengthened and sustained our ancestors. That faith was passed down to us. Like gold that was tested in fire, it was faith that Matt and I held onto. Faith was our rope! Though we didn't understand the bigger picture at the time, we TRUSTED that somehow God still had a plan for us.

You could say that we are now more aware and trusting in that Higher Power, Divine Intelligence, Energetic Resonance, or God, who knows the plan. The plan for each of us and the plan for the De Wan family as a whole unit. **APLAN4U.** Unlike the feeling of bitter unbelief, I experienced when I threw that "book" in the trash…glimmers of hope started to emerge and I began to think…. *maybe we ARE the family God uses?* Little by little, all the shattered fragments seemed to be coming back together.

CHAPTER 8: LEARNING TO HEAL

Up until 2014, I had never heard of energy healing or reiki. The only healing I was familiar with was what I knew of my faith in Jesus and the healing intercession of the saints or other such holy and gifted people. I fully believe 100% in the power of healing in this way. I have been a prayer intercessor myself since before I learned or knew anything about energy healing. I never considered myself one of these "special" holy persons, but I did start noticing over many years, that requests I made or made on behalf of others, seemed to have remarkable outcomes.

Energy healing practices are ancient. I would dare to say that Jesus was the ultimate healer and was trying to teach and train his disciples how to do this "laying on of hands." He even showed them how he could heal others from a distance, without his physical presence being there. And he did tell them that they were capable of doing these same things...and even greater things than these. (Jn 14:12)

My brave friend who shared reiki with me through a message from Evan, opened the door for a more expansive understanding of healing. She explained the basics about reiki and I did my own research from there. I was extremely discerning because of what my catholic faith taught me about the discernment of spirits. If there are good spirits, then there must also be evil spirits. In 313-327, St. Ignatius of Loyola originally wrote 14 rules (The Spiritual Exercises) focusing on "desolation" for when a person's heart feels far from God. In 328-336, a second set of 8 rules or "consolations" were written by Ignatius with the intention of assisting those who are firmly established in seeking a spiritual life. The consolations are ways we can recognize the movements of God in our lives. I'm familiar with Ignatian work and have read and studied some on it, but I'm not an expert. I know enough to get the general idea. As a Catholic, I was taught to be discerning, and that's a good thing. It's a very critical thing. When it comes to making big decisions in our lives, whether catholic or not, it is wise to reflect on our intentions from all angles. It's kind of common sense to me.

When doing my research on reiki I found that the Catholic Church is not in favor of this or other forms of energy healing. So much so that the USCCB (United States Conference of Catholic Bishops) wrote a letter on March 25, 2009, entitled: GUIDELINES FOR EVALUATING REIKI AS AN ALTERNATIVE THERAPY. It states that Reiki lacks scientific credibility and nursing accreditation and therefore warns of the danger in caring for one's spiritual health. "A Catholic who puts his or her trust in Reiki would be operating in the realm of superstition, the no-man's-land that is neither faith *nor science*. Superstition corrupts one's worship of God by turning one's religious feeling and practice in a false direction."

I can appreciate the concern the church has on this issue. Any institution can be overtaken by or infiltrated by influencers who don't have *properly ordered motivations or intentions* for healing its members. I think there is some fear and concern around reiki and other modalities of energy healing being cultish. Cults are formed when a group of people twist or distort ideas as a way of controlling people and their view of the world, usually for selfish purposes, or in this case, to pull persons away from their faith in something other than God. I would agree that's a fair concern, especially for any church organization or religion.

Intentions matter. I received reiki several times and each session was holy and sacred and healing for me. Each of these sessions were approached with the sincere intention that I desired healing from the pain of having lost a child. Over time, other hurts and pain were revealed to me in how I sometimes shared a role in that pain through the choices I made. I was learning to go within and do my inner work to face things about myself that needed love, forgiveness, and acceptance. This work was done in alignment with my faith in God. And yes, a lot of this work was spiritual. Prayer was part of the sessions, and even if it wasn't, doesn't God desire healing for us when we are seeking it? Just look at St. Paul in the bible who used to round up, persecute and have the early Christians killed!

Reiki and energy healing are not a religion. It is a method of alternative and holistic healing. Anything and any addiction, from shopping to exercise, to binge tv watching to substance abuse can take the place of God as idol worship. We go to our trained physicians when we are feeling sick, but they only treat our physical symptoms and some doctors treat mental symptoms. But in most cases the therapeutics are pharmaceuticals. Why isn't it ok to consider going to a trained facilitator of energy healing when you're feeling sick? These trained individuals look at ALL aspects of the body – physical, emotional, mental, and spiritual. They look for root causes of an illness rather than just treating a symptom. Energy healers do not take the place of doctors, but they can shed some light in areas where medical doctors are not trained. This should be ok and religion shouldn't be an obstacle to getting the help one needs to obtain healing.

My initial introduction to energy healing was with reiki. (Pronounced "ray-key.") Reiki is a Japanese energy healing technique for stress reduction and relaxation that promotes healing. Mikao Usui discovered reiki in the early 1900s. Reiki is the transference of universal life force energy to promote well-being and balance. Reiki is administered by the "laying on of hands."

I shared this energy-healing discovery with my spiritual director during our monthly sessions. It was through one particular session with her that I was led to research another healing modality and that was Healing Touch. My director was a Certified Healing Touch Practitioner, but I never asked her about it until it came up in one of our sessions. It was during an early November meeting as I was putting on my coat to leave, I happened to mention to her that my left wrist felt like I had sprained it, even though I couldn't recall doing anything that would cause the pain. She suggested I go home and put my right hand over my left wrist while meditating on it, to see if something "comes up." Of course, I was curious, so as soon as I got home, I did as she suggested. I sat in my prayer room, put my right hand over my left wrist... and waited. It only took a few minutes before a hurtful memory came up. I immediately went to my computer and started researching Healing Touch.

After a few hours of researching, I found out that we hold all our past memories, (including our joys, sorrows, hurt, and pain) at a cellular level *in our bodies*. The pain I was feeling in my left wrist was brought to my attention through the memory that had arisen from within the cells in my body. Once I acknowledged that pain and spoke some healing words of love and forgiveness over my wrist, the pain immediately dissipated. I was utterly amazed. I had just participated in the healing of my own body.

During our next spiritual direction session, I asked her many questions about what Healing Touch was and how it was different from Reiki. She said Healing Touch was scientifically evidence-based and accredited, therefore it was a much more accepted modality of the healing arts. It's a stringent program that involves taking 5 levels of training with a lot of practicum and homework. I decided I was going to give this a try. I registered for a Level I class that just happened to be taught at the UW-Madison Research Center in Wisconsin. In Madison -- where our Son Evan's life ended...was where my new life was about to begin.

There are a few other differences between Reiki and Healing Touch other than the scientific-based evidence that backs Healing Touch. Both use the laying on of hands or a light touch approach. The effects of healing can be felt even with the hands just hovering over the body or not touching at all. One of the biggest differences is in *how* these modalities are taught. You can learn to be a Reiki Master by taking 3 levels of classes in a much shorter time than it takes to learn all the techniques involved in 5 levels of Healing Touch. Reiki involves receiving an attunement passed on from a Reiki Master. Reiki origins come from the Japanese or East, and Healing Touch was developed in our Western World by an R.N., Janet Mentgen.

The main commonality they share is the transference of universal life force energy. Energy is Energy. We all have energy or our bodies wouldn't be moving or functioning.

I started learning Healing Touch in 2018 as I was finishing my certification in spiritual direction. My spiritual director was also my inspiration for participating in a 2-year Spiritual Guidance Training Program I attended at the St. Catherine of Siena Retreat Center in Racine Wisconsin. While I was taking Healing Touch classes, I also became trained in Reiki. My training in all these areas was overlapping yet seamless as I was immersed in a new world that treated all aspects of who we are as human beings.

Once I started taking all these classes my family started to notice a shift in me. My husband and daughter verbalized that something about me was changing. Matt started to become interested in learning about energy healing too. He took the Reiki training courses and we ended up taking the Master class together. As I went on to take levels 2-5 of Healing Touch, he became interested in Shamanism. Shamanism is another energy healing method. It combines Reiki with using other natural tools and techniques such as stones, feathers, crystals, and drumming and/or burning different kinds of incense, woods, or sages. It can include ancestral healing and other forms of indigenous traditions. It is a spiritual way of life that connects with nature and all of creation.

I find it interesting that in Matthew 8:27 the disciples having witnessed Jesus calm the storm said to themselves, "What sort of man is this, whom even **the winds and the seas obey**?" Now, I'm not equating that shamans are Jesus figures. But in this instance, Jesus did not pray to the Father and ask him to calm the storm. Jesus spoke directly to the elements of nature. And in John 14:12, Jesus tells the disciples that they will do the same things he did...and even greater! (And remember, that includes the suffering parts as well)

I've spent a lot of time pondering that verse. Shamanism is found in cultures around the world from ancient times up to the present day. Becoming a shaman is a life-transforming experience for anyone who is called to become an energy healer or practitioner. Matt is a shaman and my point in sharing this is that we all have a variety of gifts and when those gifts are developed and used for good, we all benefit. Matt received so much inner healing from going through the shamanic program. He was able to process and release a lot of pain that he was holding onto from Evan's death as well as other issues. Growing up as a boy he always wanted to go to school to become a forester. He loved being out in nature and dealing with the elements. He is a runner, and he doesn't let the rain or inclement weather stop him from running. He embraces the elements and nature and so the shamanic path was a good fit for him.

As I was getting healed, it was affecting him. I was becoming more balanced and calm rather than reactive and like a tuning fork, was beginning to have a harmonizing effect on those around me. One of the amazing benefits of us both being facilitators of energy healing is that we get to practice on one another and help each other maintain wellness. I am 62 and Matt is 69 and neither of us are on any prescription medications.

Any time we feel out of balance, we can do our own energy work, or we can practice on each other. On our journey together with losing a child, it has been an incredible benefit for us physically, emotionally, mentally, and spiritually. Now we want to offer our experience of healing to others in need and give hope to others, especially those who have suffered from the devastation of losing a child. Our faith has been strengthened with our knowledge and openness to energy healing, *not weakened or diminished*. And it has definitely NOT pulled us away from our relationship and faith in God. If anything, ancient wisdom and modern healing brought us to a deeper, more authentic understanding of The Divine who dwells within us.

CHAPTER 9: TRANSFORMING HOW YOU THINK & DESIGNING YOUR OWN BLUE-PRINT FOR HEALING

Losing a child is the hardest, most painful thing a parent can endure. When I say parent, I want to include guardians and grandparents or anyone who takes on the role of parenting a child. While it is very hard to get up after you've completely had the wind knocked out of you, the very best thing you can do is to get back into the saddle **while** *you are still honoring your grief.* Getting back into the saddle after losing a child is NOT moving on...it is a way of facing your grief as a part of your story now.

It is a CONTINUATION of the honoring of your grief *and honoring your child*. It is a time to reflect upon the goodness of your relationship and how to move that goodness forward into the world. They (your beloveds) are not stuck, and they don't want you to be either. Take inventory of the gifts your child added to your life and add them to create something new together that brings a deeper meaning into the world *because of them.* I truly believe they were in your life for this purpose. I know that's why Evan was in ours. Because they matter still and always will, you can birth something new through having had the experience of being their parent(s).

Remember how nervous you were thinking about the responsibility that comes with bringing a child into the world? You can tap into that same energy and think about how they changed and impacted your life forever. Their being gone, doesn't change that impact. It refines it. Fine tunes it. Aligns it with a new higher purpose now. Life isn't going to stay the same without them. You have been placed in a position to endure one of the most difficult things to bear in life. Remember, that ashes really are good and did you know that ashes are like fertilizer for soil and for new things to grow? Stay in the ashes until you don't want to be in the ashes anymore.

Meditate while sitting in the ashes and *ask your child what they want you to do now that they are on the other side to oversee and help you.* Honor your time sitting in the ashes. When it's time to get back in the saddle, like I did when Tina asked me a 2nd time to consider coming back to teach, there will be help and support along the way. Trust in your "faith rope." Take a leap of faith. And remember, you can't take a leap of faith with one foot-dragging. Tina was the one who gently and compassionately helped me put my foot in the stirrup and helped me ride again. It was a slow and bumpy ride for quite a while. That's ok. After such a big shake-up, it is frightening to start again. Others around you will continue to care for you as you start learning to get the peace and healing you need and deserve. People will reach out to steady you. Once you make the move, the Universe responds in kind. And also, remember that now your beloved child is very near – so close to you in your heart – they are trying to reach out and help you. I truly truly believe this with all my heart and I have some beautiful stories to share with you to prove this.

Receive, receive, receive the comfort, help, and support of others whom you can lean on. Then at some point - and for each of us it is different, you can start to embrace your "new life." You will be guided and led out of your darkness, like a child who has spent months in the dark womb, light will come and new life with it. Life is always asking us to let go of something. That something can be resentment, past hurts, lost dreams, a favorite job, or any number of destructive attachments. For parents who have lost a child, letting go is the ultimate act of trusting God. It is an act of hanging onto that "rope" to see that there might possibly be something more than just the ending. Hope and trust are the tools that gradually help us to endure the intervals between what was and what is to be.

No doubt your faith is shaken or even gone if you have lost a child. You might read some of this book and decide to put it back on the shelf, give it away or *throw it in the trash...*like I did when I was despairing and ready to give up hope. Maybe bits and pieces will resonate at different times or not at all. Maybe it will be a good resource that you can refer to when you need something specific.

Or maybe you will hear my voice and feel its lilting inflection of the care I am sending to your hurting heart.

I would like to provide for you, some blank pages here. They are for you to fill in the details of the feelings YOU are going through. You can color, draw, tape a photo, cry on them, or leave them blank. My intention is to allow you some space for your own tender story to unfold.

This may sound crazy, but I do this sometimes. I have a tiny little vial with a cover on it that I collect my saddest tears in. I started doing this after Evan died because I saw it being done in a movie about a dad who lost his daughter in a horrific way. The tears were used to water a new tree that was planted in his daughter's honor. I don't have an Evan tree...but I'm still saving them and I'll know when and what I'm supposed to use them for. They are my sacred salty tears. Combined with the ashes in my heart, I know something really good will grow.

I hope you consider this book like a good friend who is just willing to sit with you and hold your hand. I don't have all your answers, but I'm here for you and together we can honor your child. We will sit in the ashes, pray together, share a warm drink, and listen for their still small voice trying to teach you a new language of the heart. A language that can show you how you will travel **together** in a different way, to new avenues that will open up new opportunities for transformation and healing.

Evan with Mom

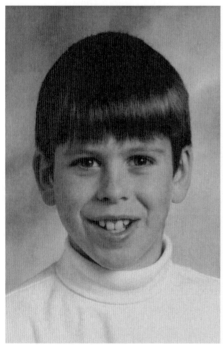

Evan, 10 years old

Evan Graduation Photo (Ambrosius)

Evan, Mike, Ann - Karate Kids

De Wan Family, Christmas 2007

Evan, Dad, Mike

Ann, Evan, Grandma - Vacation

Evan, Dad, Mom - First Communion

Evan - Graduation with Family

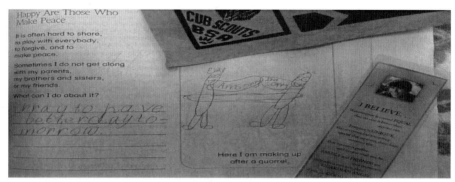

Evan, Cub Scout Neckerchief - I'm Sorry

Pandoras Box - Alexander Christopher
The Pleiidian Mission - Randolph Winters
Sourcefield Investigation - David Wilcock
Journey of Souls - Michael Newton

Edgar Cayce

Evan's Cryptic Envelope

Evan Playing with Chalk

Evan with Guitar - Christmas 2007

Sheeba

Evan with Mike C. - Wisemen

Evan with Big Sister, Erin - Graduation

Evan, Cross Country - Senior Year   Evan, DJ with Piano - Christine Tattoo

Evan Wearing Simpson's T-shirt - Christmas

Evan, Black Belt - Center

De Wan Family Christmas, 1999

Evan, Breezi - St. Pat's

I BELIEVE. . .

That everyone is created **EQUAL**,
that no-one is better than anyone else. . .

Everyone is **UNIQUE**,
that everyone has something special that separates
them from everyone else. . .

That no-one is perfect, and no-one shall ever be. . .

FAMILY and **FRIENDS** are very important,
they watch over you like a **GUARDIAN ANGEL**. . .

If you do **GOOD DEEDS** to others,
without expecting anything in return,

You will be **REWARDED** when you least suspect it.

— *Evan DeWan, 1999*

Evan, I Believe - Cardstock Prototype

CHAPTER 10: WHAT TO EXPECT AND THE UNEXPECTED

This chapter shares what I experienced throughout my 11-year journey in dealing with the loss of our son Evan. This is by no means a blueprint for what **you** will experience, but it might shed some light for you as you go through the loss of a child or beloved. It might be a starting point for the process or it might help someone close to you who is dealing with the pain of such deep loss. I'm sure there are other valuable lessons and experiences that I have not mentioned here. Each of your stories of loss is unique, diverse, and beautiful. This just happens to be mine. I've gone through 10 years and distilled my experience into one word, with a brief explanation that follows.

Year 1 – 2013 - NUMB

NUMB. Just like when you get a shock from an electric current or your hands get so frozen you can't feel them, this is how I felt in all my senses, emotions, and spirit. Looking back it was actually a gift. I don't think I could have handled the entire shock wave at one time. Like frozen fingers that gradually thaw by first getting itchy and tingly before you can get your circulation back in them, my spirit needed this protection. Another good analogy would be like experiencing surgery. You get anesthesia to "numb" any pain from the procedure you are having. My heart was protected from feeling the pain of having a huge gaping hole in my heart. I was afraid to think about the accident scene and what Evan might have been feeling or what pain he experienced. The numbness kept me from going there in my mind. After reading several books on the afterlife and near-death experiences, they say that the spirit leaves the body at or a split second before the moment of death. I can't know for sure if it's true, but I believe it is. Still to this day, it brings me comfort.

There was one really great thing that happened to me that year as my numbness was wearing off. I was hired as the part-time youth minister at St. Agnes Parish in our neighborhood. I was hired right before the 1-year anniversary of Evan's death. This was when getting back in the saddle started to feel safe and the horse I was riding began to trot around the track. I'm sure Evan had something to do with this. At age 52, I was given an opportunity to work with teens and see the impact I would have on them and how they would love and impact my life as well.

Year 2 – 2014 – LONELY

After the feeling in my limbs started coming back, there was this incredible feeling of loneliness that was with me all the time. Even when I was with my spouse, my friends, and my incredibly wonderful new co-workers at St. Agnes. I was so blessed to have a good friend walking closely with me at this time. Her name is Sandy Detry. She was always available to spend time with me. Her husband Rick walked with Matt and together they invited us over for the holidays. They took us under their wings and their simple gifts of hospitality and presence were godly. They went out of their way to do special things for us. Matt and I planned a weekend in door county for our anniversary that year and we decided to eat dinner at a restaurant they suggested. When we went to pay our bill – they had already taken care of it ahead of time. They had this planned all along.

Sandy was always comfortable listening to me talk about uncomfortable things. She leaned right in. She was a cheerleader for me and would bring me coffee as I would be finishing up a big paper that was due for one of my classes. I finished my religious studies certification program through Silver Lake College this year. It took me 6 years to complete the program because I almost gave up and quit at one point. I remember sitting in my office after hours as I was writing my required letter to the bishop about how the program helped me and my family. I still felt like a failure and a fake. I sat there for 2 hours typing and erasing, typing and erasing before I finally wrote something down.

The month of May came and both my husband and the Detrys came to watch me receive my certificate during the celebration Mass at St. Francis Xavier Cathedral in downtown Green Bay. The education I received through this program laid the groundwork for my future work in spiritual direction and energy work. This was a long-awaited dream, and I finally crossed the goal line. I especially want to thank my friends at St. Agnes for supporting me. They were truly wonderful to me. I loved every minute of working there. It ended up being the best job I ever had. The teens and parents I worked with were amazing.

Two other simply amazing and miraculous blessings came for us this year. First, we acquired our beautiful dog, Sheeba. Our daughter Ann was incessantly always talking about us getting a dog and I was never a pet person. But we ended up finding Sheeba at the humane shelter – or shall I say, she found us. She was the loneliest looking dog in the entire place. She's 10 now and was a big help in healing our hearts. The 2nd miracle was buying our cabin on Blue Moon Lake. The details surrounding this miracle awaits in Chapter 13.

Year 3 – 2015 – CHALLENGING

In February of that year, my mother had to come to Green Bay for major surgery and ended up spending a month at our house to rehab. I was able to work from home while caring for her. During that time her brother, my Uncle Jim died. It was a record-breaking cold winter that year. Mom and I had to miss Jim's funeral and my nephew Scott's wedding.

Even with my life getting busier, losing Evan was always in the back of my mind. I didn't want to talk about it all the time, and yet I did. I was not going to play this "woe is me" victim. I figured the appropriate time to share my tragedy would present itself if I needed to talk about it. One of those appropriate times came as our youth group went on a summer mission trip to Rochester, N.Y. that summer. We had to start promoting and planning these trips early in the school year so we could fundraise for these service trips.

There was one family in particular that I was drawn to that year. I found out this family had lost their dad just a couple of years prior. Both mom and dad were from my same hometown of Gladstone, Michigan. Talk about a small world. Connor was the only boy with 3 sisters in this family. He rarely spoke and kept to himself. When I found out his older sister Paige was interested in going on the trip, I asked Connor, after class one night if HE was considering going on the trip. His response was, "I'll go if you go." Here was my challenge. I had never planned or taken a group of teens to some unknown place. I've always been a homebody. I was a little nervous, but I knew I was being stretched.

As it turned out, our group was too small to fill a bus so we were able to join another parish, and the youth minister of that group (thank you Calli!) helped me with organizing and planning. She showed me the "ropes" so my anxiety lessened about the whole adventure.

The night we arrived in Rochester, we had a big group gathering to do some introductions and fellowship. One of the boys (Michael) in the other group had a birthday so Calli bought a cake to share with everyone. Evan's birthday was in a couple of days and one of my chaperones (Cassandra) happened to remember this. She approached me and asked how I was doing…and up until that point I hadn't given it a thought. But when we sat around in the big circle with a big birthday cake sitting in the middle, I could feel the tears welling up. She made sure to sit by me and she put her arms around me and mentioned to everyone that we'd be celebrating Evan's birthday too. That's when my youth group kids first knew that I had recently lost my son.

Paige, Connor, and I were together in a small group on Wednesday of that week and were stationed at a church to do some painting. At break time I found Connor sitting outside by himself on the steps of the church. I sat down with him and small talked briefly. It was a hot summer day. We sat there quietly – not saying much—when all of a sudden Connor broke the silence and asked me how Evan died. I told him, he died instantly in a car accident. Paige came out and heard what I said. They both started sharing with me how they lost their dad. We prayed together. Talking about our loved ones on those church steps was a very sacred moment. There were other kids in our group, but no one came out looking for us. Talking about our loved ones was a beautiful thing. That brief conversation bonded us together like glue and still holds us close today. Looking back, I was able to see God's hand guiding us to meet and bring us to that priceless moment. "I'll go if you go." I'm so grateful for that trip. The next year we went to Detroit, Michigan, and this time the planning wasn't so daunting and challenging for me. In fact, it was one of the best challenges of my life. I began to see that I wasn't "too old" to be a youth minister in my 50's. There were these kids and precious others who needed somebody *exactly like me.*

Year 4 – 2016 – OVERCOMING

This was the year I started feeling more confident in my role as a youth minister. I got to work with some other amazing youth ministers from our west side parishes. Not only did we see transformations in the kids who came to events, but also in the adults as well. Evan's birthday again landed on the week we were on our service trip in Detroit. On the day of Evan's birthday, we were stationed for work in an art district in Detroit. It was an area that had succumbed to crime and drugs and was now being revitalized. Matt came on that trip with us and we had asked for a sign. We got one. There was a huge concrete wall-sized mural with a *STAIRWAY TO HEAVEN* painted on it. That night, our S.H.I.N.E. mission trip coordinator, Augie, played the song Stairway to Heaven on his guitar in a tribute to Evan and us as his parents. My amazing friend and chaperone, Melissa Schmitt set that up! I can't say it enough, that working in that position for 4 years was such a gift to me. What I was so afraid of, was my greatest blessing. There was a time when I felt like a total failure as a mother – that raising teenagers was a total flop, but that changed with God putting me smack dab in the middle of teenagers for 4 years to show me my value, my giftedness in EXACTLY that role.

That year we chose the name "OVERCOMERS" for our youth group. Mandissa came out with her hit song by that same title later in the year. We chose it after some prayer and based it on the Scripture verse John 16:33, "In this world you will have trouble, but take courage, I have overcome the world."

Year 5 – 2017 – CALLED

Towards the middle of 2016, I felt this "nudge" to explore looking into spiritual direction programs. I loved having sessions with my spiritual director and the spirit seemed to be whispering to me to research programs in Wisconsin. I took another leap of faith and after some prayerful discernment, attended an open house for the St. Catherine of Siena Spiritual Guidance Training Program (SGTP) in Racine, WI. The morning of the open house I drove to Racine extra early in case Milwaukee traffic was heavy. I got there a half hour early, so I sat in the parking lot and read the Mass readings for the day. Lo and behold the Gospel reading that day was from John 14:12! (God's Greatness plan appears again!) I knew before I even walked through the door that the Holy Spirit had indeed called me there. This was the place where I did a deep dive into healing on a whole new level. It was here with these Sisters and staff that I learned to love and honor myself and my story. All of it. The dark parts as well as the light.

None of the required weekends of the program in 2017 conflicted with my work schedule so it was a pretty full year between working and attending school. I didn't tell many people that I was attending this program. I wasn't exactly sure what I was going to do once I finished the program, so I kept it private, however as the next year's work schedule was more demanding, it felt right to finish out the last summer camp and mission trip and hang up my youth ministry hat.

Year 6 – 2018 – DISCOVERY

Year 2 of the SGTP helped me shift gears in a new direction. I can't say enough how valuable this program was for me. To be loved and accepted for who I was felt incredible AND at the same time I learned to share deeply and listen to and honor where others have been on their journeys. This program was a deep dive into discovering my inner feelings and dealing with them. I was held in the sacred circle of the staff and other classmates with whom we all shared our most intimate joys, sorrows, and challenges without being judged. I never understood what self-care meant and how vitally important it is, until I went through this program. I was able to love myself more deeply, which enabled me to go deeper in my relationship with God. I think it's very true, that we can only go as deep with another as we're willing to go with ourselves. I actually heard God speak audibly to me one afternoon while sitting in the chapel while I was there.

I knew Evan had a big role in guiding me there. In my interview with 2 of the staff members at Siena, I shared that my son had passed away and I felt he was guiding me. I told them he was interested in topics like quantum physics and that his favorite movie was "What the Bleep do We Know." I told them I was interested in these things now too. I recall the 2 women slowly looking at each other and asking if it was ok if they excuse themselves for a minute. When they came back into the room, they had 3 books on spirituality and quantum physics, including the book of Evan's favorite movie! They said these books would be good summer reading before the program began in December.

It seemed they had some foreknowledge of something that I had only begun scratching the surface of. My view of the world and my beliefs were about to expand. It was also during this year that I felt led to find a new spiritual director. My new spiritual director also happened to be an energy healer although at the time I wasn't aware of that.

It was during this 2-year SGTP that I had the opportunity every quarter to have massage or reiki for some self-care. The staff would arrange to have professionals come in from the area who would offer these services if we chose to have them. They were NOT required, but optional. I discovered that SELF-CARE is not SELF-ISH. I now believe it is essential in living a balanced life. We have more to give of ourselves when we take care of our own needs. My daughter's favorite saying is, "You can't pour from an empty cup." True!

Year 7 – 2019 – HEALING

Healing, healing, and more healing. As I became more absorbed in learning all I could about energy healing and having healing experiences for myself, I shared them with my family and friends. As I went deeper, they saw changes in me. They became interested in wanting to experience healing for themselves and I was paving the way for them. My combined skills of spiritual guidance and energy healing came right before the pandemic and I think it was diving timing. Even though I got sick and ended up with pneumonia, I was able to continue my energy healing practicum by doing distance healing work after I recuperated. Getting sick was actually a blessing because it gave me an opportunity to experience some shamanic ancestral healing which revealed some amazing family history on my mother's side, which further goes to show how valuable and sacred this healing work is.

I experienced amazing healing through the shaman that trained Matt. For as long as I can remember, I have always struggled with colds and bronchitis. Even as a child when winter rolled around I could count on an upper respiratory cold. December 2019 and into 2020 were no different, with the exception that this time my cold turned into pneumonia. It was the week right before President Donald J. Trump announced on television, we were facing a pandemic. I had been to my doctor 3 times the previous week and I knew this was not a typical cold. I had shortness of breath and wasn't sleeping at night due to my cough which felt like shards of glass in my lower right lung. Finally, on the 3rd visit, I insisted the doctor take an x-ray which proved my diagnosis. I was prescribed antibiotics and a steroid inhaler and was feeling better within 24 hours.

Even though I physically recovered, my spirit kept calling me to find answers to a question I'd had for years. Why was I so susceptible to getting upper respiratory illnesses my entire life? Every winter I'd get a doozy of a cold that would leave me with a cough that would linger for months. I have never smoked, I eat healthy, moderately exercise, and get plenty of rest each night. I started to wonder if my getting sick had a hereditary element to it. So I booked a shamanic ancestral healing session with the same healer that trained Matt and me in Reiki. She was someone (and still is) I trusted and respected. It made sense to me that if we have physical aspects that get passed down from our ancestors, (blonde hair, blue eyes, etc) then perhaps other things get passed on too. I needed answers. I got them.

The shaman explained to me that we hold "grief" in our lungs. There is a famous quote that goes like this: "The organs weep the tears our eyes refuse to shed." A book I often refer to in helping me understand this connection between our dis-eases and our physical body is *Your Body Speaks Your Mind*, by Deb Shapiro. In her book, Deb explains that the heart chakra is associated with the thymus gland, heart, and lungs, hence the connection between lungs and sadness. Conflicts manifest in breathing difficulties[4] and with regard to pneumonia it states, "The relationship of breath to spirit is often seen in this illness, as mystical or spiritual experiences are not uncommon in those who have pneumonia. It can distort your relationship to the physical world, which is normally maintained by the rhythm of the breath and the distortion can act like a window through to another level of reality."

Now this shaman had full knowledge that I had lost a son. What she did NOT have any foreknowledge of was my ancestral background. During the session, she asked if she could focus on my mother's side of the family, to which I said, "yes." She did not know this, but my grandparents on my mom's side also lost a young adult daughter (Ann, aged 19) who died instantly in a car accident. (Our youngest daughter Ann is named after her.) She (the shaman) was sensing a deep loss that occurred even further back than my grandparents. *She said she was noticing a pattern of traumatic loss skipping every other generation and it felt like the kind of loss one experiences with the loss of a child or a significant family member.*

She said there were lung issues with a grandfather figure also. I shared with her that my grandpa worked on the iron ore docks for many years. He was also a smoker and he died in his late 60s of emphysema, a lung disease. There was more to the session, but the main take-away for me was the grief pattern. I was later able to verify through an aunt and by doing some online research, that my great-great grandparents on my mother's side had ALSO lost a young adult child...a daughter. Her name was Mary Ellen, but she did not

---

[4] Deb Shapiro, *Your Body Speaks Your Mind: Decoding the Emotional, Psychological, and Spiritual Messages That Underlie Illness, 1st edition,* Sounds True Publishing 2006, pg. 61, 218.

die from a car accident. She died from PNEMONIA in 1917...around the same time as the Spanish flu epidemic! Coincidence? I found Mary Ellen's death certificate online and was able to save it and get a photocopy of it.

Here I was having an ancestral healing session after having just recovered from pneumonia in a pandemic situation. Was this why my spirit was nudging me to get this healing? So it *was* true what the shaman had sensed. Every other generation going back to my great-great grandparents had lost a young adult child and the grief that was part of our heritage could have been passed on. Great grandparents – Grandparents – Me. A pattern of every other generation losing a young adult child. Could it be? I'm just asking the question.

So this is really important what I'm about to share with you. When a person receives ancestral healing, the healing is said to go back to the past, is healed in the present, and is carried through to future generations. It is generational healing of trauma for all time. In quantum physics, there is no space/time continuum. There is only now – and the past and future are perceptions of how we *observe them*. I have this simplistic way of explaining it. "Everything IS, all at once." (Past, present, and future.) We are multi-dimensional beings.

This is a very hard concept to grasp. However, now when I think in those terms, it makes more sense to me when Jesus kept telling people, "The kingdom of heaven is at hand." I think in quantum physics terms that *could* mean, the kingdom is here and now...it's not some place we go to in the future after we die or someplace we've already been in the past. Could this be possible?

Psalm 139 says how God knew me *before I was born, that before I came to be I was **already** part of God's glorious plan... "You formed my inmost being; YOU knit me in my mother's womb...My very self You knew; my bones were not hidden from you, when I was being made in secret, fashioned as in the depths of the earth." (Verses 13-15)* In seeking answers to my own healing, I wondered, could this ancient wisdom and modern healing be woven together as part of God's (quantum) plan? I think it's a fair question to ponder.

This was a huge breakthrough year for me. I have come to believe that we are ALREADY experiencing heaven ON EARTH...and many times we are given glimpses or "God-winks" as they are commonly referred to. It's that de-ja-vue feeling you get when we experience something "other-worldly" AS we are living our everyday lives. We've all had these moments of clarity haven't we?

More recently, I sought out ancestral healing to break other cycles of dis-ease in our family lineage. I received healing for birth defects, depression, and anxiety that came from my father's side of the family. Through ALL this healing, I prayed and carefully chose people whom I trusted to help me, to help my children, grandchildren, and future great-grandchildren. When dealing with the spiritual realm, one should be discerning, because I do believe evil exists as well. Our motivations and intentions for healing must always be for the highest good of all. All of the energy healers I have gone to for healing— ALL of them I know, were raised in the catholic tradition. In my mind, energy healing is in alignment with catholic mysticism. Angels, saints, the Holy Spirit, and our loved one's spirits, seem to be working together for our good here on earth.

Opening up to healing from this new expanded perspective didn't pull me away from my faith. It helped make more sense of it.

Year 8 – 2020 – AWAKENED

I went on a silent retreat with my dear friends Beth and Jill the weekend after the 2020 presidential election. We went to Siena and we had to follow the covid guidelines of course, but it was pretty much a ghost town at the center. Not much activity because of the social distancing, but what came from that weekend was incredible.

My friend Beth and I were 2018 graduates of the Spiritual Guidance Training Program at Siena. While in that program, one of the staff, Sr. Miriam Brown always spoke of this "paradigm shift" she hoped was going to happen in her lifetime. In our study of the New Cosmology, a paradigm shift would be a universal change in perspective of our current worldview. I definitely think we could be experiencing that shift right now. I did some art therapy that weekend which included making 2 soul collages. Art therapy is one of the many ways we can plumb our inner stirrings and express what our soul knows.

One of my collages has a picture of Alice in Wonderland getting ready to open the door to the rabbit hole at the bottom of a huge tree. This collage also has some writing utensils, a crystal ball with a moon and stars, and a photo of a girl who looks just like me when I was a curious 8-year-old child. The other collage has a magazine clipping of 4 small children of all different races with their arms around each other's shoulders. The children are over-looking a field of butterflies with wide open spaces. They see the possibilities of dreams and "unseen things" that are looming in their future.

It seems in the three years since I made those collages, I have gone down some "rabbit holes," and have discovered my true mission in life. I can see clearly now that all my experiences and my training have helped prepare me for such a time as this. I believe I have been led every step of the way by a very special Guardian Angel...and his name is Evan.

Year 9 – 2021 – COURAGEOUS

This year I have courageously stood my ground and protected my God-given rights as a sovereign human being. I refused to be silenced and wear a mask (except when absolutely necessary) because I had the time to do research and use my critical thinking skills to make my own informed choices. I attended the January 6th, "Stop The Steal" Rally in Washington D.C. because I felt I was guided to attend. I'm very glad that I went and was able to see with my own eyes what really happened that day. I'm not afraid to speak my truth or call out injustice. I chose NOT to get a shot that hadn't been evaluated for adverse reactions or long-term effects. I am courageous that I stood against forceful, shaming mandates that were not only illegal, but tried to cripple us under the disguise of government leadership for care and concern to-wards humanity. Some of my relationships were also crippled and damaged because of the division created by our current world view in regard to the political climate we are hyper focused on at this time in our history. I hope this damage will be exposed for what it is and that our divisions can start the collective healing process very very soon. I pray for strength and grace that my gifts be used to help others in that process.

Thank you, Evan., You taught me to sink or swim. You taught me to walk up-stream. I could have chosen to follow the culture and "go with the flow," but I remembered that even dead things flow downstream. Like Alice in Wonder-land, I was curious and had a healthy suspicion that something wasn't right, and I followed my intuition. During this time in our history, I was guided to "write it down" and I was given some prophetic words that were spoken over me, that I'd be writing a book. I have become more courageous through my journey of healing grief! Stop The Steal has a double meaning for me – on the macro level, it's about an election. On the micro level, it's about my inner joy. And....NOBODY...STEALS...MY...JOY!!! Not even death.

CHAPTER 11: WROTE A BOOK FOR YEAR 10

The word I chose for year 10 is DETERMINED. Some are calling this time in history, The Great Awakening. I like to call it the John 14:12 Greatness Plan. Maybe we're experiencing that paradigm shift. Whatever you want to call it, we are experiencing a lot of turbulence in our world today. I believe we are on the verge or precipice of something big. I believe there are going to be new opportunities for our world to experience peace and healing like never before. What I know, from having my whole world turned upside down in the ultimate turbulent experience of losing a child, is this: New things are birthed out of chaos. God can take anything (and God does) and uses it for good. The birthing process is painful, but oh so worth it. I believe my small role in the microcosm is to share my experience of how there is no conflict between what my faith has taught me and modern alternative healing. It isn't an either/or choice. It's a both/and. Faith and healing go together. They are not on opposing teams. *In my opinion*, it is in religious doctrine where the conflict lies. Healing is as ancient as humanity. It is my hope and dream that Healing Touch and other alternative modalities gain the respect they deserve on an equal playing field as complementary tools that work alongside Western allopathic medicine. In sharing my experience through this book, I hope I have shown you how my weary and desolate spirit was healed and how I not only survived but thrived through the experience of losing my child. The grief never totally goes away, but it can be fueled into a passion and can be acknowledged and honored. If you have gone through this, it IS a part of who you are now. If you are currently going through this, it is part of who you will become.

Evan's death is part of my story now. It is MY pain, and that pain has had many valuable lessons in it. It has softened my heart and tenderized it. Probably because it took a pounding, but nonetheless – it is more tender and compassionate, and I hope to share that compassion with you. I haven't lost Evan. He is with me in another form now. I have adjusted to that. I can call out his name at any time and I know he is only a heartbeat away. I am DETERMINED to help anyone that I can and I am honored to do it, because of my Evan. Did you know that the name Evan means "Young Warrior," or "Good Messenger," or "God is Gracious." This must be why we chose that name. It fits.

10-year Anniversary

On August 30, 2022, I wrote Evan a letter to commemorate our 10-year journey together. I wanted to express in writing how I/we have grown, adapted, and learned to love differently and more deeply because of him in our lives. Here is the update I wrote to him.

Good Morning Evan!

Erin and her family are doing well. There are some struggles and they could use some prayer and guidance. Family life, parenting, and marriage are hard work. Erin has been praying and asking for help. I know you are helping her. Jackson just got his driver's license this summer and Erin found him a really nice car. She and Jared are very good parents. I taught Alivia to sew a rag quilt, just like the ones I made for all you kids. She is a gifted seamstress! She is also a talented cook and helped me bake pasties for Mike's wedding. (100 of them!) Dad taught both kids to make homemade soap! They are both teenagers now. Jax plays hockey and Alivia is on the cheer team. They are both good students and they are each other's best friend. (Well, most of the time)

Mike got married in September of 2021. Bryonda is his beautiful bride and soul mate. She is a blessing to our family. And along with that blessing came her 2 young nephews, Troy, and Bradley. They are living in the U.P. so they are only 2 hours away from us, and very close to our cabin on Blue Moon Lake. Mike enjoys the beautiful scenery up north and especially in the woods at the cabin where he loves to hunt. Mike and Bry are growing in their faith and together are teaching the boys to pray. It was a miracle how they found and bought a home last summer with a huge yard for the boys to play in. I gave Mike your Bible from Mr. Kerns, your boss from Stroheim's. I knew you wanted me to give it to him. The signs you sent me were very clear. Thank you! In November they are expecting a baby boy! More to Celebrate and be thankful for!

Ann has many gifts and is very intuitive. I think she struggles with missing you the most. She definitely gets your messages and she shares them with me and dad all the time. She asked for a message around Halloween and All Souls Day – and within a few minutes she saw a bumper sticker that said, "Jesus Heals Broken Hearts." She is trying very hard to make her way in the world Evan. I am learning to take each day with her as a gift. She has a really funny sense of humor, not as dry as yours, but it's hard not to feel her joy when everything is going well for her. Without saying much more about it, I'm expecting the miracle of all miracles here. "The Family God Uses," with her as a major part of that. God has great plans for her and her beautiful heart.

Dad has finally retired from the pickle factory! He is really enjoying himself. Together we are doing energy healing, gardening, keeping physically fit and doing all we can to continue strengthening our family. Your dad is a rock star. He is my best friend and our relationship has deepened because of the storms we have weathered together. He really misses you, Evan. Our faith is unshakeable.

One of the best signs I got from you (there are so many!) was on a license plate I saw that Mother's Day as I was crying on my drive back from Grandma's house. It said: BST MOM. I knew that meant Best Mom and I knew it was from you. I hope you feel all of our love and prayers for you. It's pretty wonderful and magical to be able to communicate with you in this secret-coded way. Many people don't believe in signs and pass them off as coincidences. Not me. Never. I have gotten so many of your messages through license plates. It is the coolest thing ever. Keep sending them please.

I don't always understand how the signs happen...but the timing is remarkable. You and our cloud of witnesses, the Holy Spirit, saints, and angels, are always trying to show us love and guidance to let us know you are never very far off.

I miss many things about you Evan. You were respectful and well-mannered and you carried that into adulthood. I love that even though we may have disagreed on some things, you always listened without interruption and then respectfully shared your viewpoint. ***Honesty was one of your best virtues.*** *Looking back, I think I was very rigid in some of my beliefs and I'm truly sorry if you did not feel comfortable talking to me about certain issues. Taking the spiritual direction program really helped me be a better listener.*

As I was looking through some of your photos, I noticed our past pets, Corduroy and Autumn. I have learned through having Sheeba, the importance of pets and how dear they are to us. I know it was very hard on you kids when I decided we had to give them up. I am very sorry for that heartbreaking experience. Sheeba came to us in our time of need. Her unconditional love rescued us, not the other way around! How we got her was total Divine Providence and we ALL love her so much. Thank you for allowing me to receive the love that animals bring into our lives.

Every morning around 6 am I let Sheeba outside. We greet the day and thank God for all the gifts that will come forth in it. You are always included in those gifted thoughts. One day a few years ago I felt guided to go through your book bag and clean it out. It was mostly full of old mail, check stubs, and school schedules. I could see you were taking General Cell Biology and some other interesting science classes that involved quantum physics. Most of it was heading to the trash, but one envelope mysteriously flipped over and caught my eye. It had your handwriting on it. It was a list of some sort and in red ink, you had printed:

Pandoras Box – Alexander Christopher

The Pleiadian Mission – Randolph Winters

Sourcefield Investigation – David Wilcock

Edgar Cayce

When I saw the last name, Edgar Cayce, I knew you had a message for me because I had recently bought the book of his life story. I was drawn to the book because he was known as the "sleeping prophet" and many people were healed of incurable illnesses through his help. Along with my reiki experience, this book also helped open my eyes to the world of energy healing. Then in September of 2019 when I was taking my level 4 Healing Touch training in Minnesota, I came across a book called The Pleiadian Promise by Christine Day. I ended up getting the book because of your note! On pages 111-113 of that book, it talks about how spiritual battles need spiritual directors. Well, I become one in 2018!!! I want you to know Evan, that I have that envelope saved in a plastic sleeve. Here I always thought I was your teacher...and look who's been teaching who? Through researching the topics on that "list" I learned that many things in life aren't always as they appear. Thank you, Evan, for dropping me all these clues and signs along the way these past 10 years. They have challenged me and encouraged new growth.

The cathartic nature of writing to heal

As I continued pondering the 10-year anniversary of Evan's death, I came upon this quote from Pierre Teilhard de Chardin who was a priest and scientist. *"We are one, after all, you and I, together we suffer, together we exist and forever will recreate each other."* This quote mirrors what I wrote to Evan when I started a journal for him as a gift that I had planned to give to him. Time ran short, and I never got it to him. I had a journal for each one of our children that included some Scripture verses and some words of encouragement from me, their mother. Since Evan no longer needed his journal, I eventually took it over and started writing to him in it.

I wrote what I thought was most important for my children to know. *I wanted each of them to know that they are first and foremost, beloved children of God. And if they are creations of God, then God must have created them for some special reason.* I always told them if you do what you love, you will discover that reason... and abundance and prosperity will follow. You will have ALL you need and your work will be a JOY.

Writing has always been cathartic for me. It has allowed me to purge my feelings and emotions. It has allowed me to express gratitude and acknowledge pain. It has provided a way for me to ask questions and discover answers. *It has shown me a Divine Intelligence is listening.*

Here are some entries I added in Evan's journal since his passing:

February 6, 2015:

Evan, I sit here in the early morning hours and pray. I look at pictures of you and still find it hard to believe you are gone from this earth. Some of the past memories that weren't so pleasant, are fading. Dad had a dream with Grandpa De Wan in it. Grandpa said he sees you praying over our family a lot. I want you to be happy and loved and with Jesus in Heaven. I let you go when you went to Oshkosh for college. I knew I had to. I could see your determination which I admired. Parenting is the hardest job ever and we did our best. I wouldn't want to try dong it over again because so many times I fell short, but one thing is for certain – your dad and I loved you so very much and still and always will.

Sunday, February 8, 2015:

Evan, I felt your presence today. I hope you are receiving love from all our other relatives who have passed. I'm trying to listen and be aware of where God wants to use me. I guess it's a life-long process, this trying to discover our purpose. I know Mike and Ann need help too, but I have to trust that God has a better way of doing it and I need to get out of the way.

March 6, 2015:

These writings to you Evan, are going to evolve into a book that I will write to tell our story. You lived 24 years on this earth and the last 4-5 years of your life you were forging your own way into the world. During that time, there was much going on in your life that we were not a part of. We honored the space you needed. We didn't know your goals and dreams except for some bits and pieces. Your closest friends at that time (especially Breezi) had those precious pieces of you that we wished we could have shared with you personally some-day. My hope is that "the book" shines some light on the foundational parts of your life that we did have a part in shaping and how those parts have evolved even up until the present time. I also hope the book provides healing and sup-port for anyone struggling to find meaning and purpose in their life or how the life of a loved one who has passed away still continues to influence us.

Saturday, March 7, 2015:

Dear Evan,

How I love to say your name! I rearranged the living room recently and I put out my favorite picture of you, dad and Mike standing in front of the Fishery Pointe Cabins. Dad has the happiest smile on his face – standing there with his arms draped over the shoulders of his 2 pre-teen boys! I picked up the picture and held it to my heart. By doing that I can step back in time and feel again that happy, free time when we were vacationing as a family. I let tears slip out as I miss your gangly, skinny arms and your smile with silver gleaming braces. I whisper back to you that I miss you and love you. We have our own cabin now on "Blue Moon Lake." It's bitter-sweet without your presence there. Kind of like winning 2ⁿᵈ place in a race. There is an actual race running past our house today and it reminded me of when you ran cross country your senior year in high school. You didn't win any races, but you got the award for the most improved runner on the team. We loved watching you run and crossing the finish line. One more thing...Dad was really missing you last Saturday when he was on his way to work at the ice rink. He told me he just wanted to hear your name. He even said your name out loud in the warming shelter before any kids came to skate. A few minutes later while he was outside on the ice, he heard 2 boys talking and one called over to the other, "hey Evan!" I will close with this Scripture verse from Hebrews 12:1 that is actually written on the bottom of this journal page! "Since we have so great a cloud of witnesses surrounding us, let us lay aside every encumbrance...and let us run with endurance the race that is set before us." ~ All my love Evan, Mom

Thursday, March 26, 2015:

Dear Evan, I am home sick today. The nasty cold bug finally caught me. I've been praying for Erik with a "k" like you asked me too. Dad is in Arkansas this week and had an amazing dream last night. This actually happened! At 1:04am, Dad heard a knock on his hotel room door. He got up and looked through the peep hole. No one was there so he returned to bed. He fell asleep and had the following dream. You and Dad were together but I was on a sofa in a room that separated us by a glass wall so you and Dad could see me. Dad noticed you were sitting on a different sofa and he came to sit by you.

You were looking straight ahead so Dad could only see your profile. He didn't speak, but looked at you, hoping you would turn and face him – AND YOU DID! You told Dad you loved him and hugged him and Dad said he loved you too. Dad woke up at 3:00am. He told me the dream was very short but vivid. Thanks Evan, dad really needed that. Dad said in the dream you looked like you did in 9th grade. He said you had that goofy smile on your face when you turned to look at him. You meant the world to us Evan. I think you are doing some pretty amazing things now and I'm a proud mama. If only I had a clue, right? Let's keep praying for your brother and sister. Thank you for all you are doing and all your "connections." Later Dude ~ Mom

April 5, 2015 – Easter Sunday

Allelulia! Jesus has risen! Our Precious Jesus! Happy Easter Evan! Evan, I'm truly sorry I didn't teach you more about who Jesus is but I couldn't because I really didn't know him myself and my relationship with Jesus is still pretty sketchy. I have a lot to learn about relationships. I have forgiven myself though because I do know this: God loves me unconditionally and he already forgave me. We are helping Mike set up his new apartment today. I'll bring the holy water and a St. Michael the Archangel medal which I will discreetly place somewhere. (I wedged it behind the bathroom mirror!) Don't worry Evan, I did the same thing when you moved to Madison. I blessed your space and hid a medal in your backpack, lol. I hope to see your entire face and tell you how much I love you. I want to hug you too. I know it will happen.

Monday, April 3, 2015

Good morning Evan, I'm taking over your journal. I'm also taking Taryn, your friend Ryan's daughter to Vacation Bible School this week! I'm really excited about that.

That was my last note to Evan in his journal. When I started putting this book together, I was asked by my writing coach to compose a letter to Evan to commemorate the 10-year anniversary of his passing. I shared some of that letter in the previous 10-year anniversary chapter but here is the remainder of that letter to Evan and what I still miss about him.

I really miss your love of music. We always had music playing in our home, either on our stereo or one of us playing on our pianos. (We had 2) Music fills a home with beauty and joy. My own parents had a love of music, and music was really my first encounter with "The Divine." Remember when dad wired speakers into all your bedrooms and you all got to take turns picking out what soft music you would fall asleep to? We had everything from classical to lullabies to silly camp songs! I know your love of music was everything to you. Your tattoo of the piano keyboard spoke of the importance of music in your life. Mike and Ann each have a tattoo of a rose in honor of you to signify their love for you. Dad and I have you engraved on our hearts forever.

I love how you grew up to be so frugal and live simply. You did not have a lot of "stuff." You focused more on living life rather than collecting material things. And another thing I especially loved about you was this incredible ability you had to make all around you feel welcomed. You were inclusive and people were drawn to that. You had so many friends probably because you didn't judge people on outer appearances. You noticed beauty within. You had a deep respect for life. I found a report you wrote in high school about your views on respecting life. You did not believe in abortion and I remember how proud I felt reading your words that were compelling and well researched. Abortion has been a hot topic this past year and just so you know, Roe v Wade was indeed overturned on the federal level in 2022! That just means that the power goes back to the individual states to decide. I believe that's where the power should be. From there – I guess it's between the individual person and God. That's where all our decisions should be anyway – in my opinion. It looks like a step in the right direction. Maybe we should consult God in all our decisions, right?

I miss your voice. I miss saying your name as well as hearing it. I just love your name so much. According to The Dictionary of Patron Saint Names, by Thomas W. Sheehan, M. Div., your name means "God is Gracious," or "Young Warrior." When I was working in ministry, I would always find a way to do an exercise with retreat participants on knowing the meaning of their name. God calls us BY NAME. (Not by a pronoun) We are all children of God collectively, but individually we all have unique names. I always stressed, especially to children and teens how very important it is to know who you are and to whom you belong. Just as important is to know where you've been so you can decide where you're headed next. It goes back to that core foundational message I wrote to you in your journal about discovering your purpose and mission in life. It was such an honor to have chosen your name, Evan. It's one of the most special privileges a parent gets to make. No one else gets that honor. Evan John De Wan. Sounds poetic and angelic, I think. I believe you have stayed true to your mission. You ARE a gracious and powerful messenger, especially from where you are now.

For other parents who have lost children, this would be a tremendous exercise to help you heal. Reflect on your child's name, research its meaning, and then write it all down. Doing this could reveal to you some significant messages and healing for both of you. Writing has been very cathartic for me my whole life, but even if you're not into writing, this small exercise could truly reveal some beautiful insights for you. Nesting is also a structure of writing that plumbs the body/mind connection and allows words to bubble up naturally. You start with writing one word on the first line. On the second line, repeat the first word and then add another. On the 3rd line, write word 1 & 2 and add word number three...and keep repeating this pattern. This exercise is like priming the pump and your writing will begin to flow like water. Here is an example:

Evan

Evan has

Evan has taught

Evan has taught me

Evan has taught me to

Evan has taught me to honor

Evan has taught me to honor death

Evan has taught me to honor death as a portion of the complete circle of life. All Lives Matter. All Deaths Matter. Each person leaves an imprint on the world. Each person affected the entire world in some unique way like a snowflake that adds to the beauty of creation.

Writing brings me to a place of clarity because I can SEE my thoughts in front of me on paper. I can go back and look at my writings and see how my beliefs have evolved or changed over time because of the lens I may have been looking through at the time. I can recognize patterns and then I can acknowledge what beliefs HAVE NOT changed. These beliefs become my steadfast Truths.

Evan loved to write. Actually, all my children do. They have all written poetry to express themselves at one time or another. I think Evan may have loved writing music more than words while he was in his early adult life, but I saved some of his writings because they were so good. When he was 14 (in 2002) he wrote a poem called *"I BELIEVE." (This was the poem we made into bookmarks and gave out at his funeral.) I had written a poem in 2000 entitled, "TRUTH."* These were both such beautiful pieces of prose that complimented one another, that we had them framed and hung in our front entryway. Now they are hanging in my prayer/healing room.

Evan, I will close out my letter with these words of thanks to you. The experience of being your mother has been a privilege and I'm so grateful for all you taught me. I'm much more open and respectful towards other people's beliefs and I'm much braver than I ever thought possible. My faith is stronger, and I understand better that darkness and light complement each other. Challenges and struggles were opportunities to shape and form my character like iron that sharpens iron. I have nothing to fear when I remember that Divine Love is holding ALL OF US. The Divine dwells within me and that's where all my answers can be discovered. Love is holding you and Love is holding me. You are forever in my heart. Thank you for all the lessons you taught me WHILE on earth as you did in heaven. (And still are!) You will never be forgotten as well as our loved ones who have gone before you. We carry your light and love within us. As WE have been transformed by your life, we help transform others. As we become at peace with death, we perpetuate a vibration of peace throughout the world. Let there be Peace on Earth, and Let it begin with me. Because of You.

All my love, Mama Bear

CHAPTER 12: HEALING TOUCH

The Healing Touch Program was founded by Janet Mentgen, BSN, RN, HNC, HTCP/I. She lived from 1938-2005. Her motto was "Just do the work." Here's the classic definition of Healing Touch (HT): It is an energy healing therapy in which practitioners consciously use their hands in a heart-centered and *intentional* way, to enhance support and facilitate physical, emotional, mental, and spiritual health and well-being. HT utilizes light or off-body touch to clear, balance and energize the human energy system in order to promote health and healing for mind body and spirit. HT is used to *complement* (not replace) conventional or allopathic health care. HT is one of the most respected and valued integrative therapies in healthcare facilities where holistic methods are practiced. Healing Touch is offered as an alternative healing therapy at hospitals such as UW Madison and the Mayo Clinic. It is practiced worldwide and is used extensively in all nursing professions and settings. It is the only alternative healing therapy to date that is accredited by the American Nurses Credentialing Center (ANCC) Commission on Accreditation since 2011. HT is also endorsed by the American and Canadian Holistic Nurses Association. (AHNA and CHNA) Healing Touch is considered a worldwide leader in energy medicine due to its successful history since 1989.

The definition given by Merriam-Webster for allopathic medicine is this: *"relating to a system of medicine to combat disease by using remedies such as drugs or surgery which produce effects that are different from or incompatible with those of the disease being treated."*

It occurred to me that this allopathic "system" seems to only combat or treat the *symptoms* of a disease. What I like about energy medicine is the uncovering of symptoms to treat the ROOT CAUSE of the dis-ease. Rather than suppress the symptom with a drug, why not try discovering the cause that brought the symptom on in the first place? How about we offer unconventional, alternative, holistic, osteopathic, or homeopathic methods *along with* conventional allopathic treatment in an effort to reach optimum wellness?

That is what Healing Touch teaches. It attempts to offer healing for **all** aspects of us as mind/body/spirit human beings. Our creator designed our miraculous bodies with the ability to heal themselves. When the body is placed in a relaxed state, whether resting or sleeping, it is poised to obtain optimum healing. All of our memories are stored within our bodies at a cellular level. When we feel an ache, pain, depression, or anxiety – it is our BODY trying to communicate to us that "something" inside needs attending to.

The life of a healer

Starting in 2018, I chose to learn as much as I could about Healing Touch – this new way of healing was introduced to me by my spiritual director. I was both eager to learn and to heal. My ultimate goal was to be able to help others heal from their pain and trauma. I officially became a Healing Touch Practitioner (HTP), completing all 5 levels of training on May 22, 2022.

I was drawn to practice Healing Touch in particular because of my own skeptical attitude towards energy healing. I suspect there are thousands of hurting people who could benefit from alternative energy or naturopathic healing, because of my sharing this experience. I happen to think the timing is perfect for alternative healing to be considered as an option in our post-pandemic era. Mental health issues were already a crisis and isolation mandates further exacerbated anxiety and depression worldwide. The lockdowns had a devastating effect on millions of children and adults around the world.

A Healing Touch session typically lasts an hour. Each session is as different and unique as the client. A first session takes a little longer due to taking a medical history background, signing a consent form, and answering any questions a client may have. A session begins with an Intake for the client to determine what the long and short-term goals of healing will be. A practitioner never determines this. Energy healing is client driven and the practitioner is there to assist and guide them on their healing journey.

The client stays fully clothed and gets comfortable as possible on a massage table or recliner. A pre-assessment of the client's energy centers and biofield is noted by the practitioner. The practitioner will determine which method or combination of methods is best suited for the client's intentions based on the pre-assessment and Intake. The session comes to a close when the methods are finished and a post-assessment has been taken. The session is closed out with feedback between the client and practitioner. This feedback is useful for continuing a growth plan that is in alignment with the long and short-term goals. If the session was helpful to the client, they may choose to make another appointment. The frequency of appointments depends on the client and their trauma or illness. Referrals can be made at this point also.

All sessions are a sacred holding of the most intimate parts of a person's story. I never ask a client to share anything they are not comfortable disclosing and part of my consent form explains my responsibility to hold their sacred story with the utmost confidentiality and professionalism.

If a client needs help beyond the scope of practice of the HT Practitioner, then according to our practice of ethics, a referral might be made for another form of healing that would be beneficial for the client. Wanting what's best for the client on all levels of healing, whether it be physical, emotional, mental, or spiritual is paramount. Letting the client decide and participate in the entire process helps empower them in making their own decisions in regard to their health. I also want to stress again, that energy healing of any kind IS NOT a replacement for your medical doctor(s). Both forms of healing therapeutics have a specific value.

So that is what a healing touch session looks like. Before I began my training, I received healing touch as often as I felt needed. The time in between sessions will be different for everyone. Just like going through the stages of grief when you are processing it, time is needed to integrate the changes that are taking place within you. A lot of short-term goals can be addressed along the way as layers are removed and your long-term goals are met.

In 2017, 5 years into my healing journey, I was enrolled in the Spiritual Guidance Training Program and was deepening my relationship with Self, God, and others. During that period I learned to accept and love myself unconditionally as best I could. My faith grew in knowing that God loved me with ALL my failures and weaknesses. I learned to embrace ALL those pieces of myself that I was trying to eradicate because I thought they were "bad." I learned to love those aspects of my humanity and to appreciate that in certain instances, they served me very well. (Like my tendency to be bossy!) I learned when to allow those aspects to be put to good use and to temper them with other aspects of myself that were equally important.

From there, in years 6-7 of my journey, I moved from receiving energy healing into becoming a facilitator of healing for others. It was during this part of my journey that I experienced the most profound healing around the loss of Evan. It happened during my Level III Healing Touch training in Madison where I was able to release some of the remnants of grief I had still been holding onto at a cellular level in my body. I call it the "Ugly Cry" session. I thought I had already cried out all the tears by then. Nope.

I was nervous that Friday about driving myself to Madison for that weekend's training. Within a few miles of coming close to my exit, a HUGE Blue Moon Semi truck came alongside me on the highway and pulled ahead of me. I knew it was a "divine" escort because it took me right to the exit where I needed to turn off before it pulled away.

Then on Saturday while I was on a walk for my lunch break outside, something quite remarkable happened. As I was walking, I could hear a cardinal singing very loudly like it was calling for my attention. I couldn't see it but kept hearing it while I walked around the campus. As I cut across a sidewalk path to get back to class, I looked down, and there at my feet was a dead bird. I knelt down with sadness in my heart to see the little bird, and at that very moment, I heard the cardinal again. Still kneeling, I looked up and there facing me, way up high on the very tippy top of a tall tree was the bright red cardinal singing. It was looking directly at me. The red, LIVING cardinal above me, and the little dead bird at my feet.

At that moment I received a message. I knew IN MY HEART, that both life AND death are precious and to be honored. I felt Evan's presence was palpable and I shared this experience with the group when class resumed. They were amazed as well.

Sunday, our final day of the weekend training, I was partnered up with Mara, a retired R.N. who was like a grandmotherly figure to me. It was my turn to receive healing and as she started working, I could feel anguish and grief rising up from my feet, getting stronger and stronger with momentum as she kept working up towards my chest. When she got to my heart it was as though the damn burst open and the gushing cries nearly choked me. Mara held my sacred space and allowed what needed to happen. It was like a tidal wave had finally crashed. It was an incredible feeling that I will never forget. A complete emptying of all the grief and anguish I was still holding inside of me.

Now it was late in the afternoon and time for the class to wrap up. I was a snotty mess, but I had enough time to compose myself. Mara stayed with me until I was ready to join the group and gather my things for the ride home to Green Bay. The ride home was just as incredible. The sky was looking ominously dark so I quickly got in my car as it was starting to rain. Within a few miles it was pouring SO hard, I was contemplating turning around. It was as if the sky had just mirrored my gushing emotions that spilled forth in a torrential rain just a short while before! I slowed down and kept driving with my windshield wipers on at the highest speed. When I got on the highway, the rain gradually started tapering off but was steady all the way to Fond du Lac. As soon as I got to the Highway 41 turn-off, I saw a double rainbow across the sky. I pulled over at the next available exit and got out so I could take a picture while I was thanking the Universe for responding to me with such incredible love. The pouring rain with the double blessing rainbow was an absolute reflection of what I had just experienced in my body in that Healing Touch session with Mara. And here I am today, still rejoicing in the rain and the rainbow, the red cardinal, and the little sparrow, as I share all the treasure with you. God. Never. Disappoints. It's all part and parcel of our beautiful stories.

As I reflect back on this part of my healing journey, I'm humbled that even though I never wanted to go with Matt to Madison to see the crash site of the accident, I was led back to the city where Evan's death occurred and at the same time, it is the city where I sustained the deepest healing of my life. With absolute certainty, I felt Evan was guiding me back to the place of my wounded heart. I've learned that each of our healing journeys, should we accept to go on them, contain some interesting twists and turns. I'm starting to realize that the healing journey, or our "in-between phases of life and death process" is just as much to be honored as the bookends of life and death. It's ALL a beautiful story. All of it. Each day is to be cherished and contains hidden gems within.

What I'd like to share with you next is how I was asked to give Healing Touch to a client who was getting ready to depart from the earth. This was probably the most profound session I have given a person to date. I think it might bring us full circle to my life as a healing facilitator.

For confidential reasons, I will call this client Suzy. Suzy started coming to me for HT sessions upon the referral of a friend. It was also during this time that I had just finished my Level 4 HT training. Suzy was nearly 70 and was diagnosed with Neuro-Endocrine cancer in the Spring of 2019. In her words, she considered herself a "spiritual catholic." She had a deep faith and was open to alternative methods of healing. She had tried many other alternative therapies which all provided for some easing of her symptoms. She was proactive in trying a blended approach to wellness. She followed her doctor's advice and kept him informed of her successes in dealing with pain management and her slowly progressive weight loss. She seemed very in tune with her body and was doing a good job balancing her chemo, supplements, exercise, diet, and prayer. Our first session was in September of 2019, and we continued regular sessions right up until her last session which occurred 6 days before her passing in early 2020. For her last session, she requested I make a home visit as she was too weak at this point to leave her home. I offered her a "distance session" but she really wanted me to come in person to her home where she lived alone. She said, "I just feel so good when you're praying over me."

I thought she might be transitioning to her "heavenly home," and felt humbled and honored to go offer her whatever comfort I could. I was a little nervous as well. Even though I sensed her transitioning, I still asked God for a big miracle to heal her because I know God has this kind of power. I also know God gives us what we ask for, so maybe we just don't understand that sometimes the healing comes *through* death. It's just a wondering I have because God sees a much bigger picture than we do. I believe God *did* give Suzy her miracle. It just looked different than she or I may have expected.

When I arrived at her home, Suzy had just taken her chemo pill and she was feeling very nauseous. She asked that our session focus on helping relieve the nausea. She also shared that she had been holding onto a secret for most of her adult life. I privately wondered if there was a connection between this "secret" and the cancer that was "eating her alive." It really didn't matter, what was most important was that after performing her pre-assessment I could feel that her bio-field, the energy surrounding her physical body, was just inches from her skin. An average/normal bio-field is typically 2 feet or an arm's length from the body. I knew her energy was being drawn inward which can be an indication of a person who is actively dying.

A pre-assessment is done in Healing Touch to assess the spinning of the chakras. The body has 7 major chakras (also known as energy centers) that align through the center of the body from the top of the head, which is your crown chakra, to the base of the spine, which is referred to as the root chakra. Healthy chakras, or energy centers, indicate balance, harmony, and well-being of the body. No spinning sensation or movement would indicate some sort of disturbance or compromise of the energy field.

I prayed over Suzy and felt guided to administer the HT method that assists the body with transitioning. She fell into a deep sleep. I noticed an extremely deep exhale about midway through the session, which seemed to indicate a releasing or "letting go" of some sort. Her breathing then returned to normal. As the session was winding down, I intuitively received the words, *"Work to do on the other side."*

I made sure to ground her and myself as the session ended. There was no feedback because Suzy was resting so peacefully. The optimum environment for the body to heal itself is when the body is at rest, so I felt assured she was healed of her nausea which had subsided enough for her to rest. The HT work had achieved the success of her intention. "Just do the work."

These were my observations with Suzy. This was the perfect example of how alternative therapies such as Healing Touch, are meant to work alongside medical treatments and are not intended to replace them. I would also like to reiterate, that God can and does perform miracles through ANY type of healing action, whether allopathic, homeopathic, or supernatural, whether through the hands of an M.D. or the hands of a Healing Touch Practitioner or through an instantaneous healing with no human person around. The Spirit moves where the Spirit wants with unlimited power.

Two days after our session, I sent Suzy a text to see how she was feeling. She sent me an image of the praying hands. A few more days passed when the friend who referred Suzy to me, let me know of her passing. I hope that healing touch helped Suzy. I think she is helping me now...with her *"work to do on the other side."* Thank you Suzy, for allowing me to journey with you toward the end of your earthly life and for allowing me to share this portion of your story with our readers. Our stories connect us. Our stories help each other heal and not be so afraid.

I am SO grateful for how I was raised in the catholic tradition with parents who were not rigid in their beliefs and allowed me to explore and question my faith as I needed. I am grateful for the gift of my faith. A faith that is not beholden to a set of rules, but for a faith that allows me to constantly deepen my relationship with God, Self, and Others.

Healing Touch is what was presented on *my* path and it is where I felt more secure, knowing it had scientific evidence along with accreditation backing it. I think there may be a lot of people like me out there who have either lost a child or experienced deep loss, who are looking for alternative healing and just need a trusted, secure on-ramp to begin that process. I combine my spiritual guidance training and the deep listening skills it taught me, with my Healing Touch and other skills to offer healing to anyone in need. Healing Touch is where *my path* unfolded and if I feel another healer is a better fit for a particular client, I can and will definitely give a referral to the many other healers I now know. There is help for everyone!

CHAPTER 13: FAITH THROUGH LOSS

Throughout the past 10 years, I've kept track of some special signs and un-explainable moments that lead me to believe that Evan's essence or spirit is alive and well. I truly believe life continues on the other side of the veil (and I'm guessing if you are reading this book, you do too!) and if we're open to it, we can receive messages, ask for help and stay in communication with our loved ones if we choose to. I'm not sure if it's Evan's individual spirit, or if it's a collective holy spirit, (I don't have all the answers!) but whatever it is, or how-ever it works, I have most definitely received communication from the other dimension(s) of reality, heavenly realms, or whatever you choose to call it. All I know is that something remarkable does happen and our beloved children and loved ones passed, try to let us know they are with us in another form.

As I approached the 10-year anniversary and the writing of this book, I can honestly say I am truly at peace. Like any painful lesson, we have 2 choices. We can either remain stuck in our grief, or we can learn to navigate the pain while discovering what lessons are in it. In time we can move through the stages to the other side where deeper vistas of joy and understanding exist. Like my wise brother Jim who is an avid hunter once told me, "Everything dies so something else can live." My ever-growing faith has grown deeper because of my work in energy healing. I may never have ventured out into that arena if it weren't for losing Evan. (and remember, I haven't really lost him.)

When one person starts changing their vibrational energy in a household, the dynamics and energy fields in that space start changing and affecting others around them. I started changing from the inside out, with my healing experi-ences, and "Evan-tually" my family wanted to try some healing alternatives too. It's like a tuning fork where everyone starts coming into harmonic resonance.

Dr. Rupert Sheldrake, an author, biochemist, and researcher in the field of parapsychology, explains this phenomenon as "morphic resonance." I read several of his books as I began studying energy medicine. The basic meaning of morphic resonance is that within a species, certain behaviors can be felt, known, and experienced by others of the same species. The behavior modifications can take place as far away as other continents. It is more commonly known as the 100th monkey syndrome. The 100th Monkey theory tells us how the behavior of one group can spread to all related groups, even though some groups may be physically separated and have no means of communication with each other. This can partially explain how "distance" healing or perhaps Intercessory prayer works. Remember that thoughts are energy and thought precedes form. "Let there be PEACE on earth…and let it BEGIN WITH ME." I believe that as each person heals, this morphic resonance creates an energy frequency that flows outward.

If you want to learn more about changing form, behavior and morphic resonance, a good book to read is one by Rupert Sheldrake, *Science and Spiritual Practices, Reconnecting through Direct Experience.*

I'm going to highlight a few of the "signs" I've received, to show you the many varied ways you can look for communication with your beloved.

It was a Friday, February 1, 2013. It was the 5-month anniversary of Evan's death. There was still this somber feel blanketing our home, especially since it was just Matt and I in our empty nest. I had just enough energy that day to physically plan and prepare a meal where we could sit down together. It was also Super Bowl weekend, and we were invited over to our friends, the Detrys, to watch the game. This had been an annual event for us in the past.

In preparation for Friday's meal and Sunday's game, I needed to make a trip for groceries. I wanted to pick up a bottle of wine for our friends and I decided to pick out a bottle of wine for our dinner that night as well. I went for my usual Riesling, but then I thought to myself, "Why not try something new?" So, I put the German Riesling back on the shelf and walked up and down the aisle one more time. It was the color of the bottle that first struck me…like the dark night sky. The brand was Bridgeview, and the name of the wine was Blue Moon, an Oregon Riesling. The label on this cobalt blue bottle was dotted with silver stars and a crescent moon. Beautiful. And since I like Riesling, it made its way into my cart as I went to get my groceries.

Later I started preparing dinner so it would be ready when Matt came home from work. I wanted to do something nice for him and I wanted to do something "normal" for us. When it came time to eat, we prayed, and it was very quiet. We didn't say much as we ate our meal. Matt started saying he was feeling very sad and asked me if I knew what day it was... I said I did know it was the 5-month anniversary...

He began to reminisce aloud about the night of Evan's death...remembering the football game and the sky with the blue moon that night...THE BLUE MOON – Holy Cow! I jumped out of my chair and cried, *"Oh my God! I forgot something! I have to show you!"* (I finally made the connection!) I literally ran over to the refrigerator and grabbed the bottle of Blue Moon wine and showed it to Matt. We looked at each other and in our hearts we knew we had just received a message from God, from Evan, from the Source of love surrounding and holding us. I had no idea why I bought that particular bottle of wine, but God knew and was reassuring us that all was well. Matt, who usually doesn't drink wine, had a glass with me that night to celebrate this very special message and how it connected to our "anniversary of the heart."

This story of the Blue Moon wine was later shared on a pilgrimage bus. Matt and I went on a 3-day pilgrimage to visit the Marian Shrines in Wisconsin. It was a bus sponsored by the Green Bay Diocese. One of the persons on the bus was the editor of The Compass, the diocesan newspaper. After hearing my witness story, she asked if I'd be open to an interview to share the story in the newspaper. Of course, I was, especially if it could help someone else on their healing journey. The interview took place in my home in October of 2014 and the next month the story was published along with a photo of me holding Evan's graduation picture while sitting next to the bottle of wine. I mentioned to Sean Schultz, who did a fabulous write-up, that this was not the end of the story...

A series of 2 miracles happened next. The first is how we acquired our pet dog Sheeba and the second was how Sheeba led me to pay attention to an ad for a property for sale.

Matt had been traveling a lot for his job and our youngest daughter moved back home. She was working at a doggy daycare center because she LOVES dogs. I was never a huge fan of owning a pet. We owned a German Shepard when I was growing up and I was afraid of the dog. Ann was incessant about telling me her dog stories from work and was always showing me pictures of them. She kept insisting and chiding that we should get a dog. When she was younger we'd go to the humane shelter "just to look," so she could get her "fix." Well...I finally agreed that we could go look, but I had no intention of coming home with a dog.

It was a Monday when we went to the Green Bay Humane Shelter and there was an overflow of dogs for adoption. That day there was a sale on any dog that was 12 months or older – half price, I suppose to get them in homes. We cruised up and down every aisle and even took one dog outside. High energy male who immediately jumped up on me. No deal. We went back in and walked up and down the aisles 1 more time...when we noticed her.

We must have missed "Sheena" the first time around. She looked like a German Shepard...all curled up tight in a corner with her ears plastered down... looking like the saddest dog we'd ever seen. She grabbed my heart immediately. We both wanted to see her. She had to be carried to the visitation room by the volunteer staff person because she was so scared.

Ann and I sat in that room for a very long time with Sheena curled up in the corner under a chair and terrified. She wouldn't lift her head or look at us when we talked to her. Her trust in humans must've been broken. At one point, I thought we should try an experiment. I asked Ann to leave for a few minutes and then come back. When Ann came back into the visitation room, we got 1 tail wag and so we tried it again, this time, Sheena slightly lifted her head. That was it. My heart overruled my head and I instantly made the decision to bring Sheena home with us. I was not leaving without her. We filled out all the paperwork and changed her name to Sheeba (Ann's idea!) and carried her to the car to bring her to her new home.

Sheeba turned 10 on July 22nd, 2 days after Evan's birthday. She is a JOY...and SHE really rescued us. The sadness in her was a reflection of how devastatingly sad we were without Evan. By Monday evening, we had a new loving companion in our house named Sheeba. She is a Shepard mix, about 45 pounds, beautiful, and the perfect companion for us as we were healing. Little did I know that Sheeba would play a part in our next miracle.

Blue Moon Cabin

Sheeba came home with us that Monday and on Tuesday Matt left town on a business trip. Sheeba was getting acclimated to our home, but those first 4 days were worrisome. She barely ate anything, and Thursday was the first day she was able to keep her food down and did not throw it up. She was starting to respond more and trust us. We were keeping a pretty close eye on her – I was home during the day to monitor her well-being and she was sleeping with Ann at night.

I suggested to Ann that we go out for a quick dinner and thought Sheeba would be fine with us being gone for a short time. But when we got home Sheeba must've had separation anxiety. She had "messed" on the living room rug and chewed up one of Matt's slippers. I had a couple of organized piles of papers on the kitchen table but thought it was kind of strange that only 1 piece – it was The Compass Newspaper – was chewed and strewn all over the floor. Nothing else on the table was amiss. Because of my job in ministry, I received a free copy of the paper and brought it home. It was the previous week's paper and a "for sale" ad, for a cabin, had caught my attention, so I put it aside thinking I would take a second look before tossing it. The ad was in color and was placed in the front of the newspaper, not in the back with the rest of the ads. The cabin was located in the U.P. (Upper Peninsula of Michigan) which is where I grew up.

When Matt and I married, he LOVED going to the U.P. to visit my family and he LOVED the north woods. He always wished he could own a cabin in the woods, but he really never thought it would happen. I didn't know this at the time, but after Evan passed away, Matt told a co-worker that he gave up on that dream of owning land with a cabin in the woods. I never liked camping or "roughing it." My idea of camping was at the Holiday Inn, and I was verbal about it! The thought of keeping up 2 places wasn't very appealing to me.

So back to Thursday evening and the mess in our house! We got everything cleaned up and I went to the local pet store to buy a kennel for the next time Sheeba would be left alone. Sheeba ended up loving that little space and she slept there at night with the door open. I think it made her feel safe. I still had not thrown that newspaper away. Why was I keeping it? I looked at the cabin ad again. It looked like "a dream." It was on 20 acres of land and was fully furnished. We had previously been looking at RVs because all my siblings own them and had invited us to camp with them, especially after losing Evan, but nothing seemed to pan out.

I didn't think we could afford this cabin when I looked at the price, but I noticed it had a Green Bay phone number to call for more information. Friday, the next day I called the number. Calling is free and we could afford that, so I did. It's a LONG story...and I could dedicate an entire book to just that, but here's the shorter version of what took place.

A man named "Al" answered the phone. I introduced myself and said I had seen the cabin ad and wanted to know more about it. He said he and his wife, Chris, owned 2 other homes besides the cabin and it was getting to be too much to maintain all 3 in their retirement years. I explained to Al that I was from the U.P. and all my family lived there.

Al steered the conversation to faith, saying he and his wife were members of St. John the Baptist parish in Howard. I told him I was currently the youth minister at St. Agnes Parish in Green Bay. I knew and worked very closely with the youth minister from his parish. His voice got excited as we were talking – he knew my friend & co-worker in the vineyard, Jody. Jody and I were the oldest (we liked to say "seasoned") youth ministers in the diocese.

As the conversation continued, we found we had other things in common. Faith was extremely important to us and was now established. I also knew Al and Chris's sister-in-law, Theresa. I worked with her in my previous job at NWTC and the 2 of us sometimes went to Mass before work in the mornings. All these connections made our conversation flow easily as we circled back to the cabin and I decided we'd set up a time to see it. Al gave me the contact information of the realtor they hired from Iron Mountain, Michigan, and said it was easier for her to give us a showing rather than he and Chris running back and forth from Green Bay. Before hanging up, Al told me not to hesitate to call again if I had any other questions about the property.

I called the realtor immediately after hanging up with Al and she had availability the very next day, Saturday. I booked a time with her, even without having talked this over with Matt yet! Yikes! First, we get a new dog on Monday, and on Friday when he gets home, I'm telling him we're going to look at a cabin in the woods. Talk about a surprise-filled week. Sheeba chewing up that newspaper ended up being a very good thing. It got me moving...you could say it was *providential*.

When Matt got home Friday afternoon, I filled him in about Sheeba, the mess, the newspaper with the cabin ad, and that I had set up an appointment to see it the next day. He verbalized that this would be a waste of time, but since I had made all the plans, he knew there would be little point in trying to dissuade me. We got up Saturday morning to freshly fallen snow and were set to meet Carrie, the realtor, at a gas station about 9 miles from the cabin. From there, we would follow her "into the woods."

Carrie explained there were 2 ways to get to the cabin and she suggested taking the more scenic route. Because of the curvy, hilly road combined with the fresh snow, we had to drive between 20-25 mph. As we turned off the main road, the icicles hanging from the trees were thick. The morning sun was peeking through, and sparkling droplets were beginning to form in a magnificent display of winter wonderland. Reflected in every direction were prisms of glistening light that danced as if the forest were alive. It was absolutely breathtaking! It looked like the magical winter scene out of the Land of Narnia from the C.S. Lewis movie, *The Lion, The Witch and The Wardrobe*.

In the movie, 4 young siblings discover Narnia while playing hide and seek. Narnia is a perpetual winter wonderland in all its snow-covered glory. Did I mention that Matt LOVES winter? We were mesmerized by the beauty of the day and decided that even if the cabin gig was a bust, our day was not at all wasted because of the beauty surrounding us.

It seemed to take forever to get to the cabin as it **was** very deep in the woods. It was in a very private setting and we liked that. As we pulled into the long driveway, we came to a clearing where the cute little Lincoln log cabin proudly and humbly stood. We noticed the wildlife lake was just starting to freeze over. The realtor informed us that the property was completely surrounded by state land, making this cabin the only property on the lake. It looked and felt like a slice of heaven. Then we went inside.

The look on Matt's face was priceless. I was behind him, and I literally saw his jaw drop as his head swiveled to take in a panoramic view of the rooms. Large windows opened up the view to the lake. There were all the luxuries of home but on a smaller scale. All the furniture, everything in the cupboards, the lawn mower in the shed...EVERYTHING was included. It was "move-in" ready. Matt was trying to find something wrong with it. He couldn't. It was absolutely perfect.

I did find one item, however, that the owners may have wanted to keep. I noticed a sign in Italian on the woodshed and asked what it meant. Carrie said it meant "lake of the deer." I asked if that was the name of the lake and she explained that it was not. The DNR actually has jurisdiction over bodies of water and assigns a number to a lake such as this one, so she said we could name the lake whatever we wanted if we were to own the property.

After being completely satisfied with what we saw and after all our questions were answered, we told the realtor we'd get back to her if we decided to make an offer. She said there were other interested parties so not to wait too long. I leaned in and told her with sincerity, **"This is more than a business deal, and if it's meant to be, it'll be."** We were definitely interested but needed to let the idea settle in our minds and then figure out a game plan. Financing the cabin would take some creative maneuvering and prayer.

Our excitement on the drive home was palpable. Matt talked about the lake and started throwing out ideas of what we could name it. He tossed out a few names which didn't resonate with either of us...and then all of a sudden, his eyes widened as he blurted out, "How about Blue Moon Lake?" THAT WAS IT!!!

The dream was set in motion and the rest are details of how everything lined up for us to purchase this cabin. It was like the stars and the moon were all in alignment. Everything fell into place. Prayers were answered and more healing was to come. There were so many God-Winks! We ended up meeting the Carlottos, the owners who shared with us that they were "praying for the right family" to buy their treasured cabin built on hallowed ground. We closed on December 27, 2014, in Iron Mountain.

The Carlottos came to the bank closing and afterward, they showed us another route to get to the cabin. When we got there, they had a gift for us. A bottle of blue moon wine and beer! By this time in our relationship, I had told them our story about losing Evan. The realtor knew the story as well, and she was crying tears of joy over this transaction, that was *"more than a business deal."* It had been like I mentioned to her, "meant to be." We gave the Carlottos a key and said they were welcome to stop by and visit anytime. We felt blessed beyond anything you can imagine and we gained 2 new friends in the deal. We still get together for dinner with them every year and catch up with talk about the cabin and our faith.

Acquiring the cabin on Blue Moon Lake was probably the biggest surprise ever. It was a miracle for sure. However, a cabin would never replace our Evan. We never had a chance to just be "friends" with him. What the cabin provided was a sacred space to heal and it was close to my family up north. We are located 40 miles from my parents, 40 miles from my sister's hunting camp, and as of September 2021, we are 40 miles from our son Michael and our new daughter-in-law's home in Iron Mountain. Mike met and married a beauty from Iron Mountain. Can you believe that! Our cabin is smack dab in the middle of all of them. It is hard for me to comprehend how God has orchestrated such a beautiful story and continues to heal and use our family...and connected us to another Blue Moon believer...

How the Blue Moon Story continued and connected us with 2 other families through sets of twins...

When I returned from middle school summer camp in June of 2015, the parish secretary had written down a message for me. It was from a woman named Mary who wanted me to return her call. She had read the Blue Moon article of my interview in The Compass and wanted to meet with me. She and her mother had been praying for our family ever since the story was printed. She thought our stories were somehow connected and asked if we could meet for lunch. I had never met this woman, but I was intrigued and agreed to meet her and her 90-year-old mother. We met at Pizza Ranch on Wednesday, July 1, 2015. We talked for 3 hours as Mary poured out her life story. Mary was just a few years older than me, and a delightful, faith-filled person. She shared with me her love of children and that she always dreamed of having a large family with 10 kids. She also had many health challenges. She had survived breast cancer as a teenager, but still suffered from the effects of her treatments. It was a miracle that she was able to have children at all and ended up having 2 beautiful sons. But because she had so much love to share, she begged God for a healthy body and more children.

She knew she had to surrender control to God. Besides her health, there were other things out of control in her life. One night when Mary felt she was at a breaking point, she found herself crying out to God in St. Louis church in Dykesville. It was while she was there in her hour of need that she heard God speak to her. *She heard God tell her she would have twins.* There was no mistaking this message. She said she heard it clearly and she was still holding God accountable even after all these years. Now she was past child-bearing years and remembered again what had been clearly stated. *You will have twins.*

Now God didn't say she would "give birth" to twins...God just promised them to her. The remarkable twist to this story is that this night in Dykesville, in 1985, there was a Blue Moon. That's why when Mary read my story in The Compass, she had to connect with me and ask for my prayers. She was CERTAIN God would keep his promise through this sign.

Of Mary's two sons, one was married and had started a family. She thought perhaps the twins would come through her son Chip and his wife Katie who already had one child but were hoping to enlarge their family. I agreed to pray for the highest good of all concerned. God always answers prayers, but the way in which they are answered can be full of surprises! I let Mary know that! She was thrilled and she said she would keep praying for the healing of my family as well. We still needed it very very much.

- So let's recap: I meet Mary and her mother Carol on July 1, 2015.
- I agree to pray for Chip and Katie to have twins. (they do not know we are praying for this, btw)
- I put them on my prayer list, LITERALLY.

Now let's fast forward to December 26, 2015. It was a very sad day because our son-in-law's father had just passed away that morning. I went over to babysit our 2 grandchildren in the afternoon while my oldest daughter Erin and son-in-law went with his family to the funeral home. When they returned, I heard Erin softly mention something about *Chip and Katie... expecting...* What? Jared "shushed" Erin and when I asked what all the fuss was about, they told me that Jared's younger brother Chip and his wife, who's name just happens to be Katie – had just found out they were expecting TWINS. Jared gently scolded Erin for letting this slip, but I told them I would tell no one, and then in the next breath I told them that I had been praying for Chip and Katie to have twins. *But not THAT Chip and Katie!* I told Jared I was totally serious and when I got home, I took a picture of my prayer list and sent a copy via text to Jared. I found out his brother's twins were due in July of 2016.

So now I was praying for an actual set of twins and a potential set of twins, whose parent's names were both Chip and Katie. How bizarre...and I had to laugh out loud! I said to myself, "God, this is the wrong Chip and Katie!" I added the new parents and twins to my prayer list. And I just kept praying.

The new year of 2016 had arrived. January, February, March...no word from my friend Mary about her Chip and Katie having twins. But I DID hear there was going to be a healing priest from Uganda coming to Our Lady of Good Help, the Marion Shrine near Dykesville and so I decided to bring my prayer list and go.

It was kind of a dreary cold day and as I was waiting on the church steps to get in, my cell phone rang. It was Mary! She had just received the news that morning from her daughter-in-law Katie that she was pregnant and she and Chip were expecting twins in August! I had not talked to Mary about the other Chip and Katie yet, so she had no idea how the story was unfolding. My head was reeling. I told Mary that something very unexpected happened and I would call her immediately after the healing Mass. When I called a few hours later we were both talking and crying in utter amazement of what God was doing. Wow...talk about keeping promises! Talk about double Blessings!

Just when you think this story can't get any better, it does. My cell phone rang on July 11, 2016, just as I was pulling into my driveway. I had just finished my Wednesday holy hour at the adoration chapel. It was Mary and she sounded breathless as if she was running a race. I was the first person she called to tell me her daughter-in-law just had an emergency c-section and gave birth to twin boys! Mother and babies were doing well, despite the boys' early delivery. Praise God! Mary had to make other calls, so we hung up and I immediately called my daughter Erin to share the good news with her. Erin's response was "Oh My God!" She had just gotten off the phone with Jared, who told her Chip and Katie were also at the hospital, the same hospital getting ready to deliver their twins!

Lo and behold, both sets of parents delivered their twins on the same day and at the same hospital! And here's the topper. July 11th is the feast day of St. Benedict, who was a twin to his sister, St. Scholastica. You just can't make this stuff up. Maybe there really is something rare and magical about Twin Blue Moons!

Mary passed away in April 2022. Her poor health finally gave out. She was a beautiful soul and a prayer warrior. It was an absolute honor to know her and be a small part of her story. God kept his promise to her. She *did* get her twins and I made sure to write the story down and pass it on to her family who up until her death knew nothing about our prayers. About four months later, I received a phone call from the other Katie who had just read the letter and we set up a coffee date. I had the privilege of meeting Mary's daughter-in-law recently and it was such a blessed visit. It's still so amazing to me how the Blue Moon brought Mary and me together. But it was more than that. It was the steadfast faith of 2 women who fiercely loved children, especially their own. And who believed that with God, ALL THINGS ARE POSSIBLE.

There were so so many other signs and wonders that I will probably write another book just on that topic alone. I want to continue to inspire others that good and beautiful things are woven from the threads of **all** our circumstances be they happy or sad. Woven together, the details of our individual sorrows and joys are the highlights of our unique sacred stories which connect us in our collective human experience. I believe ALL healing contains elements of forgiveness and this last special story tells of how 2 brothers worked through forgiveness. One from heaven and one from earth. And how I, their mother was chosen to mediate that message.

"You can only go as deep with another, as you're willing to go within yourself."

This is what was taught in our Spiritual Guidance Training program. I believe this to be true with all our relationships. I've learned to be more PATIENT… especially when it comes to helping others on their healing journeys. We are all unique and take different paths. We all process differently. Our son Mike was a year and a half younger than Evan. In many ways, Mike looked up to his big brother, but in some ways, he felt let down and there were some loose threads left hanging between the two of them at the time of Evan's passing. Sibling rivalry is a very natural occurrence, but death can steal the opportunity to make amends or say things that need saying.

Around the same time I was learning reiki and healing touch, I was being shown the subtle energies and how to communicate by using my intuitive senses. It seemed to come naturally to me and I followed my inner guidance to take a class in mediumship training. This training proved to be very valuable in helping me pass on a message from Evan to his brother Mike, in an effort I believe, to tie up some loose ends and to help Mike on his healing journey.

Even though I learned mediumship skills, I don't do readings for clients. The skills I learned became of immense value in helping me decipher subtle messages. One evening at our development circle, a small group of us who had been through the mediumship training did an exercise together. We were to connect with a "spirit on the other side," and then write down everything we were sensing so we could share it with the group to see if anyone could "claim" the message that was given. We always started this work with prayer. There were about 8-10 of us. We meditated and got silent for about 10 minutes. When the time was up, we wrote down a list of everything we intuited. While in this meditative state, we were trained to use all our senses or "claires" to help interpret what a particular spirit might want to share. Here's what I wrote down verbatim on my list: (I still have my list btw)

- Young male, see him around '20s
- Upper head – pain sensation
- Feels REALLY personal (serious, sensitive, reverent, sacred)
- Felt a surge of deep penetration across my shoulder, chest, and heart
- Felt such warmth, to the point of sweating – Love message
- Heartbreak – really hard on me

- (Sorry) for causing so much pain
- Deep inner struggles
- I asked that an image be shown, and in my mind's eye I clearly saw a yellow-gold cub scout neckerchief

When it was my turn to read my list to the group, nobody could claim the message or associate the clues with someone they knew who had passed. I was almost the last person in the group to share, so we skipped over my list and went on to the next person. The teacher of the group came back to me after we had finished and asked me to read my list again, which I did. As I read it out loud, it dawned on me (and her at the same time) that this was possibly a sign from my own loved one.

It "felt really personal" because it was. IT WAS EVAN. "Young man in his 20's" was Evan. He died from blunt force trauma to his head and chest. The heartbreak and sorrow were in alignment with what it feels like to lose a child so traumatically. The deep inner struggles – I didn't know at the time of Evan's death, but his best friend Breezi later shared with me how Evan was battling with depression and wanted to make some changes in his life. The yellow-golden cub scout neckerchief was the only thing that didn't make sense to me. Yet.

It's really hard to explain how I felt recognizing Evan communicating with me through this experience. To comprehend that your child – or loved one – can communicate with you through thoughts, smells, bodily sensations, inner knowings, and images – seems impossible, yet I know what I experienced and it was real. I took my "list" home and every few days would look it over to try to make more sense of it. It seemed like maybe there was more.

It wasn't until about 2 weeks later that I kept thinking about the image I saw. The yellow-gold neckerchief. Matt and I were cub scout leaders when our boys were in scouts at St. Joe's when they were younger. I thought I had kept one of their uniforms...in...my...cedar...chest. The moment I remembered this, I ran to the bedroom and opened my cherished cedar chest. My father-in-law handmade it for me and I kept my precious keepsakes in it. As I opened it, I saw about halfway down on the right side, the corner of that gold neckerchief.

I carefully lifted and put aside all the special keepsake items that were neatly stacked on top of it. The item that was directly on top of the neckerchief was Evan's First Communion workbook. I gently picked up his book and when I set it on the floor, it *slipped out of my hands and fell open to page 35 which started a chapter entitled, "The Eucharist Is About MAKING PEACE."*

I paused for a moment as the book mysteriously lay open in front of me. There was a picture of a young boy looking downward (as if sorry) and across on the next page it said: "Happy are those who make peace." The lesson further stated "Sometimes I do not get along with my parents, my brothers and sisters, or my friends. **What can I do about it?** In the space provided was Evan's 2nd-grade handwriting response that said, "**_Pray to have a better day tomorrow._**" But what made me gasp aloud was the drawing that accompanied Evan's response. He drew 2 stick figures. The larger one had "Evan" written above it. The smaller stick figure had "Mike" written above it. Evan's stick man had a speech bubble and in the bubble, it said, "*I am sorry.*" Mike's little speech bubble said, "*I'm sorry.*" The stick figures were hugging with extra-long outstretched arms around each other. At the bottom of the page in big bold words were, **Here I am making up after a quarrel.**

I knew without a single doubt in my mind, the neckerchief was a clue that was meant to lead me to this message. A message Evan wanted me to deliver to Mike.

The only problem was that Mike and I were still struggling together in our relationship. Sometimes he would get angry with me and we wouldn't talk for periods of time. I knew I had to be very very careful **how** I would deliver this message and **when.** This is when I really leaned into my faith, and I prayed every day. I took that golden yellow neckerchief out of the cedar chest and put it under my pillow. Each night, I prayed that the Holy Spirit would **show me an open door** as to when to give Mike the message. Some nights I'd tie the neckerchief around my neck and sleep with it, and every morning I laid it across my pillow, smoothing out the wrinkles just as carefully as you would see a priest smoothing out the linen on the altar at Mass. It became my sacred morning ritual.

Sometimes we have to be really, r-e-a-l-l-y patient when waiting for Divine Timing. But wait I did. And then the day arrived. About six months later I got a call from Mike one morning on his way to work. He said he had some things bothering him and he wanted to know if he could stop by after work and talk.

I knew this had to be big because Mike is very private. I kept asking Spirit all day, "Is today the day Lord?" "Will the door be opened for me to walk through and deliver the message to Mike?" Is he ready to receive it and really believe that this was a message from Evan for him?" "To tell Mike he was truly sorry and to ask for his forgiveness?"

Mike came over after work and it just so happened that he and I were alone in the house. I don't remember exactly how our conversation started, but Mike brought up something about his job and feeling angry about how he was being talked to and treated at work...and missing Evan...(*door opened*)...I remember saying to him, It's ok to move on from a job if it doesn't feel right or you're not being treated well...and then I told him I had something to show him.

I went to my bedroom to retrieve the workbook and the neckerchief and asked Mike to follow me into the prayer room. We sat down and I said I knew Evan wasn't always there for him when he needed someone to look up to. I verbally affirmed for Mike that I knew Evan wasn't always nice to him when they were growing up and the last time they saw each other ended up on a sour note. We talked about how hard it is to grieve for someone you are angry with...and the guilt you carry because that person is no longer around to even try resolving the issue.

It felt like a sacrament was taking place, except rather than taking place in a church confessional, it took place in our home as I showed Mike page 35 of Evan's workbook, and I explained how I got the message I was about to share. I cried as I watched my precious middle son start to shake and cry as the healing tears that had been held in for so long started to flow. Six months was worth the wait. I would have waited for as long as it took for Mike to be ready to hear and receive Evan's apology. God sees all and knows our hearts. Had I tried to force giving Mike the message any earlier, I would have let my own selfish desires abort the mission. I love *God's plan* for us. He is never early and never late. If we listen, we will hear his voice and know when to go through the sacred doors as they are opened for us. Mike believed the message came from Evan. Mission accomplished. There was no obstacle, space, or separation between heaven and earth big enough to keep this message from coming forth. Love Never Fails.

I still have the list, the workbook, and that yellow-gold neckerchief. I may give it to Mike to put in his cedar chest. It was an old chest that Evan junk picked, and my brother-in-law Harry refinished for Mike. But I'm still holding onto it because I've been praying for one more special miracle. Maybe it's wishful thinking, but I'll wait and see what keeps unfolding for this family of ours. The Family God Uses.

CHAPTER 14: JOY AND HOPE

When I look back through my journals, I have had so many encounters with The Divine, I could write a book alone on just those stories. "How do I Love Thee?" "Let Me Count The Ways,"

I think when we are open to continuing a relationship with our loved ones, we have to realize that once they are on the other side, the relationship changes, and along with it the communication changes. A new Love Language, if you will, takes place. I try to see this Loving Essence communicating with me everywhere on a daily basis. When I ask, I receive. When I reflect daily, I can see where I was being guided, nudged, comforted, loved, and corrected throughout my day. Catholics call this **The Examen** which was instituted by St. Ignatius of Loyola who had a major conversion while reading the lives of the saints as he recovered from a serious battle wound. Visionary cosmologists like Judy Cannato, author of *Field of Compassion, How the New Cosmology Is Transforming Spiritual Life,* calls this **"Awareness."** Judy states: "I am not my thoughts. I am the Awareness that observes them." This awareness is quicker than a reflection. When you are *aware*, you are noticing or observing ***in the present moment*** that you have Christ Consciousness and are experiencing The Divine in the now, present moment.

Many times, when I'm witnessing to someone, Spirit usually shows up to validate what I'm saying and the person(s) I'm with gets to see a glimpse of "heaven on earth." One time on a walk with my two young grandsons we found 2 dimes in random places. We were on a scavenger hunt and started talking about the treasures we were finding. Upon finding a feather, our conversation gravitated toward angels. That's when we found the 1st dime. We literally asked the spirit out loud for another dime to be shown to us and you can imagine the excitement we felt when we got back to the house and in our mailbox was another dime!

This is the language of the heart I'm talking about! All I know is that when this "magical mystery" happens, I feel a JOY that is hard to explain and hard for others to believe UNLESS they see and experience it too. It is a joy that cannot be stolen from us, and I cling to these moments when experiencing difficult and challenging times. It is a child-like innocence that is not jaded by worldly cynicism. It's a contagious joy and I can guarantee that when you remember those moments...*where* you were, *what* you were doing and thinking at the time, *who* you were with, *you KNOW* you received a "response." And the resulting feeling is JOY.

 This happens a lot in our family. We are always finding dimes when we need a hug from the spirit world. We make a big deal of it. When we find a dime, we take a picture and send a text to everyone. This is how we spread our JOY!

Pierre Teilhard de Chardin has a famous quote: *"Joy is the infallible sign of the presence of God."* He also said: "*We are not human beings having a spiritual experience. We are spiritual beings having a human experience.*" Pierre Teilhard de Chardin (May 1, 1881 – April 10, 1955) was a Jesuit priest, scientist, paleontologist, and theologian who believed in a blending of science and Christianity and was known for his theory that man is evolving mentally and spiritually toward a final spiritual unity. I believe de Chardin's thinking was ahead of its time.

His writings were banned from being printed until after his death because they were so controversial. ***"Someday, after mastering the winds, the waves, the tides and gravity, we shall harness for God the energies of love, and then, for a second time in the history of the world, man will have discovered fire."***

Read Matthew 8:27 about Jesus calming the storm again. From de Chardin's perspective, we too as human beings are discovering our inherent power and authority as co-creators. It is my opinion that *"harnessing for God the energies of love,"* is what I am practicing when I'm giving a Healing Touch session. Again, here's the classic definition of Healing Touch: It is energy healing therapy in which practitioners consciously use their hands in a heart-centered and *intentional* way, to enhance support and facilitate physical, emotional, mental, and spiritual health and well-being of body, mind, and spirit.

Perhaps energy healing modalities such as Healing Touch and other alternative methods, are moving us closer to that "spiritual unity" that de Chardin talked about. We are finding answers about the relationship between *life and death* with the help of ancient wisdom and modern healing. 'I don't even think the healing should be labeled as "modern." I think the healing is as ancient as the wisdom. Energy healers are just now gaining the equal attention they deserve to share their spiritual gifts in a world where spiritual healing is sorely needed. We are getting our foot in the door and gaining credibility among conventional medical doctors as a viable option for healthcare treatments.

*Blue Moon, A Story of **Everlasting** Love,* seems to mirror the bigger picture as reflected in the Glory Be prayer. "GLORY BE to the Father, and to the Son, and the Holy Spirit. As it was in the beginning, is now, and ever shall be, ***world without end***. Amen." Love never ends and Love never fails. Death does not prevail. Life goes on in another form. In time, we can learn to let go of the familiar form that embodied our beloveds and enter into, more deeply, our new life together in a spiritually profound way where we are never separated. Coming to the realization that we actually have this choice, can offer us "deep hope." And hope is *always* something worth clinging to.

"The future belongs to those who give the next generation hope." - Pierre Teilhard de Chardin

In the Bible, it says that Jesus sent the disciples out two by two, and miracles like meager amounts of food were multiplied to feed thousands. Years ago, when I first started teaching religious education to 9th graders, I would ask them on the first day of class what they wanted to learn that year. One student in the front row, Joshua, raised his hand and said he wanted to know more about miracles. That's a topic I LOVE to talk about.

In energy healing language, it is called "manifesting." In spiritual language, it is called "co-creating." It's the intention behind the language that is most important. We often get hung up on the words when it's the loving intention be-hind those words that matter most. When I worked in ministry I once offered to pray and "send healing energy" to my boss when he was feeling under the weather...he reminded me that, we call "that," *GRACE.* Without getting into doctrinal theology, isn't it basically the same thing? I think the loving inten-tion behind the words is what matters most. It's just a different language. The intentions of the heart speak their own language. Both words are acceptable, one is just more "science-y."

My main reason for writing this book was to share some of the miracles I have witnessed over the past 10 years that were part of my story. I wanted to share how God is using me and my family through our healing journey, so you can feel free to ask your questions and find your answers. Together, from both realms of heaven and earth, we are able to continue to deepen our relationships and find healing. In *Love Is Stronger Than Death*, by Cynthia Bourgeault, this profound deepening of relationship goes beyond the grave in her experience as well. Her loss was that of a beloved confident and her book demonstrates her yearning to keep that connection after death, but not in a clingy way. It greatly impacted how I learned to view death as an opportunity to achieve what couldn't be done any other way. It truly helped me recognize there is a higher form of human love.

I want to deliver to all of you, a message of hope...a message that Evan put on my heart—that New Life is possible for you as well. When you suffer the loss of a child, you are faced with many choices you never thought you'd have to make. The biggest choice being that you can have a New Life, or you can choose to sit and stay in the ashes forever. Choosing the New Life path does not mean that you don't sit in the ashes for a while...you need those ashes to help nourish the ground beneath you. The pain you felt and continue to feel is so deep because the depth of love in your heart for your child was anchored there. It's not meant to disappear or go away. The person whom you loved made a permanent mark on your heart that stays there forever.

The world is a better place for having had Evan John De Wan in it for 24 years. For me it's a no-brainer and here is why. I was 28 when he was born. If I live to be 100, I can say I had nearly a quarter of my life spent teaching him, minus the 28 years BEFORE I became his mother, which leaves me with 48 years he gets to teach me. That's the simple math of it. I'd say I got the better deal.

We all have something unique to offer the world because I think we are all reflections of The Divine. Evan sparkled just like a star in the heavens. His dry wit and humor, his sense of adventure was contagious and he was just plain fun to be around. He was intelligent, organized, and handsome. He was musically gifted and I know Ashlyn loved the "moving song" he wrote just for her. He was an encourager and told people the truth (Breezi) that they should believe in themselves and in their dreams. Evan wrote this poem in 8th grade and it pretty much sums up what he believed.

I believe that everyone is created EQUAL, that nobody is better than anyone else...

I believe that Everyone is UNIQUE, that everyone has something special that separates them from everyone else...

I believe that no-one is perfect, and no-one shall ever be...

I believe that FAMILY and FRIENDS are very important, they watch over you like a GUARDIAN ANGEL...

I believe if you do GOOD DEEDS to others, without expecting anything in return, You will be REWARDED when you least suspect it.

I believe that too. Except that most parents want to believe their child is perfect...so I like to say we are all "imperfectly perfect." Evan definitely made his impact while here and left his legacy with me to share our story. I truly believe, just as he trusted me to give his brother Mike the message of forgiveness, he wanted me to write this message to the world.

I believe his arrival on July 20, 1988, was divine timing, and it is my opinion that his departure was divine timing too. Whether I understand that or not right now, is none of my business. It was his journey and I happened to have the honor of being his mother on that journey. Thank you, God, for the gift of our son, Evan. It took the journey ***of his life and his death*** to enlarge my heart.

It brought me to the brink of despair to show me how *authentic* love cannot be snuffed out. In fact, his death re-ignited the spark of passion and the Holy Spirit stoked the flame so we could create something new together.

On July 20, 1969, the Apollo 11 mission was accomplished when man first walked on the moon. It was a monumental time of discovery in our world. It was a pushing of the boundaries when the astronaut Neil Armstrong quoted, *"That's one small step for man, one giant leap for mankind."* Nineteen years later on that anniversary, a star was born, and his name was Evan. That was my "labor day," when he came into the world.

Then on Labor Day, September 1, 2012, under the light of a Blue Moon, his journey ended with his mission accomplished. July 20th is also the feast day of St. Appollinarus who was a noted miracle worker. The moon shows up every night. The Blue Moon on the night of September 1, 2012, was special and unforgettable. By the light of the moon, I was led down a path of discovery, pushing past old boundaries of faith and healing, into a new expansive world of understanding.

I didn't find all the answers, but the Blue Moon provided just enough light to find what I was looking for. Everlasting Love. Moons, Miracles, Mystery, Wisdom, Healings...JOY!

Until we meet again Moon Man,

~All My Love, Mom

How Do I Love Thee? (Sonnet 43)

<u>**Sonnets from the Portuguese, Elizabeth Barrett Browning (1806-1861)**</u>

How do I love thee? Let me count the ways.

I love thee to the depth and breadth and height

My soul can reach, when feeling out of sight

For the ends of being and ideal grace.

I love thee to the level of every day's

Most quiet need, by sun and candle-light.

I love thee freely, as men strive for right.

I love thee purely, as they turn from praise.

I love thee with the passion put to use

In my old griefs, and with my childhood's faith.

I love thee with a love I seemed to lose

With my lost saints. I love thee with the breath,

Smiles, tears, of all my life; and, if God choose,

I shall but love thee better after death.

John 16: 21-22

"When a woman is in labor, she is in anguish because her hour has arrived; but when she gives birth to a child, she no longer remembers the pain because of her **joy** that a child has been born into the world. So you also are now in anguish, but I will see you again, and your hearts will rejoice, **and no one will take your joy away from you.**"

ACKNOWLEDGEMENTS

To ALL who have helped me find answers...

To my son Evan, for leaving me "clues" and sending me signs when I needed them.

To my husband and forever friend, Matt. For your Support and mostly for your Groundedness. While I was always dreaming of what could be, you were "boots to the ground" getting things done!

To all my Ancestors, Saints, Angels and Loved Ones Passed for their guidance and wisdom. Especially my grandparents Gust and Julia Almonroeder and my Great Great Grandparents, Walter, and Julia Collins who both lost young adult children and for my grandparents John and Tracy Stock who through their prayers, provided a bedrock of solid faith as my foundation. For maintaining your JOY as you endured many hardships in life!

For my parents, Peter and Nancy who were "perfectly imperfect" and modeled to me how good parents should raise children ~ With a village of aunts, uncles, and cousins, you ALL did it with a sense of fun and a healthy dose of fear! I wouldn't trade my childhood for anything! It taught me how incredibly important family relationships are. (Still learning...)

To my stepmother Mary who also recently joined "the club" with the loss of her daughter Debbie. Thank you for loving Dad and for taking such good care of him.

To my stepdad Tim, for winning some of your hardest battles that will be gifts to his children and grandchildren for years to come.

To my children, Erin, Evan, Michael, and Ann – all of you have been my greatest teachers and greatest Joys! You challenged me to grow **and go** where I never thought I'd be. To Jared, our gem of a son-in-law, and Bryonda, a jewel of a daughter-in-law and for our beautiful grandchildren, Jackson, Alivia, Troy, and Bradley and soon to be baby boy De Wan! May our family continue to blossom through God's Grace.

To my siblings, Jim, Joan, and Jeanne. They don't come any finer. And to their spouses and families and especially my nephew Scott Richer – you know why!

To our friends Sandy and Rick Detry, who walked alongside us during our darkest hours, weeks, and years after Evan's death. Your practical actions and steady hands kept us moving forward. You both always knew what to say and how to be. You are two of the classiest people I know – and super fun to take road trips with!

To my spiritual director, Kathy Welhouse for both her unconventional AND traditional prayer as well as her keen sense of compassionate listening.

To my dear dear friend Mary Van Nuland, whom I discovered through my development circle friends from Golden Light Healing. For your Healing Touch wisdom and experience and for being my go-to person when I need a session!

To Amy and Dave Wilinski, Owners of Golden Light Healing...for sharing your vision, light and love with the world.

To my dear friend Nancy Saladino, an answered prayer when I needed to find another student to practice with and for Mara, my Healing Touch partner when I experienced "the ugly cry." Thank you both from the bottom of my heart.

To Pamela Searles, my mentor who helped me cross the finish line in 2022 and become a Healing Touch Practitioner!

For all my friends and co-workers in the "vineyard." There are too many of you to name, but each of you helped shape my experience of Christ's love for one another.

To my special friend Mary McDonald, grandmother of one set of the "twins," and to "Suzy," both who have recently passed on and who I know are "cheering me on" from the other side. Thank You. Thank You.

For the best neighbors EVER – John and Shelly Siemering. FOR. ALL. THE. PRAYERS.

To Frank, Aaron and Jan Gibes – whose lives and story intertwined with ours through the loss of their beloved Josh.

To my dear friend J.B. – who took a risk in coming to me with a message from Evan…you got the ball rolling…

To Ann e King, my gifted friend who made Evan's bookmarks and for your beautiful sense of style and grace.

To Ron & Jane Garrity, Evan's Godparents. For so many things – cars, vans, trucks and a lifetime of laughs and the best 4th of July displays that rivaled downtown Green Bay. And especially to Jane for introducing me to the "chapel in Robinsonville."

To Julie, Kathy, Mary, and Jane. Girlfriends in God and Partners in Crime. To Beth and Brenda and all the "Lectio Ladies" who meet on Freedom Fridays!

To my coach, editor, marketer, and publisher, Tracy Ertl, whom I met in June of 2022 by divine guidance. For Lori Preuss and all the team at TitleTown Publishing for performing your design magic and editing skills over all my technical mistakes as a first-time author. I hope to meet you and thank you in person someday.

To John Blaha, Becky Bond, Andy Zakowski, The Compassionate Friends, my co-workers at NWTC and all who helped me in any way with love, support, meals, and magic on this journey.

To Breezi, whom Evan believed in… and who showed me what can be done… **when you believe in yourself…**

And lastly, but most important of all, **TO ALL YOU LOVELY SOULS WHO HAVE LOST CHILDREN**, no matter the age or the circumstances, …I dedicate this song to us all, Robert Vincent - The Ending (Official Video) - YouTube, *because none of us really and truly knows the ending. May you be healed and blessed and may no one ever steal your JOY!*

CITATIONS

Your Body Speaks Your Mind, Deb Shapiro, pages 61 & 218.

5 Stages of Grief, Elisabeth Kubler-Ross, MD, https://www.verywellmind.com/five-stages-of-grief-4175361.

David Kessler, Found of Grief.com, World's foremost expert on grief and loss, https://grief.com/the-five-stages-of-grief/.

Finding Meaning, The 6th Stage of Grief, David Kessler, david@grief.com or 818-762-7901.

Life Lessons, Two Experts on Death & Dying Teach us about the Mysteries of Life & Living, Elisabeth Kubler-Ross and David Kessler.

On Grief and Grieving, Finding The Meaning of Grief Through The 5 Stages of Loss, Elisabeth Kubler-Ross and David Kessler.

Love Is Stronger Than Death, Cynthia Bourgeault.

The Myth of Divorce Following the Death of a Child, https://www.taps.org/articles/21-1/divorce, author Stephanie Frogge.

Jean Galica, M.A. LMFT, Licensed Marriage and Family Therapist, www.jean-galica.com.

The Compassionate Friends (TCF), Support group for parents who have lost children.

(ch.8) https://www.ignatian spirituality.com/making-good-decisions/discernment-of-spirits/rules-for-discernment/.

Science and Spiritual Practices, Reconnecting Through Direct Experience, Rupert Sheldrake.

Quotes by Pierre Teilhard de Chardin, https://teilharddechardin.org/teilhard-de-chardin/teilhards-quotes/

Field Of Compassion, How the New Cosmology is Transforming Spiritual Life, Judy Cannato